JERRY V.

GOING

UNDERCOVER

Secrets and
Sound Advice
for the
Undercover
Officer

PALADIN PRESS
BOULDER, COLORADO

Going Undercover was written in memory of James Mark Bray (1953-1982). Better partners, or friends, don't come down the trail.

Going Undercover: Secrets and Sound Advice for the Undercover Officer
by Jerry VanCook

Copyright © 1996 by Jerry VanCook

ISBN 0-87364-862-5
Printed in the United States of America

Published by Paladin Press, a division of
Paladin Enterprises, Inc., P.O. Box 1307,
Boulder, Colorado 80306, USA.
(303) 443-7250

Direct inquiries and/or orders to the above address.

Contents

Preface

While *Going Undercover* was created primarily as a working guide for undercover police and private security officers, the applications for the system it presents are hardly limited to those professions. All of the techniques described, with certain modifications that should be obvious even to the novice, may be employed in other areas of life. Much as Japanese businessmen adapted Miyamoto Musashi's classic text on sword strategy, *Go Rin No Sho* (*A Book of Five Rings*), and altered the tactics into an approach to the world of commerce, the strategies contained in *Going Undercover* may be employed to gather intelligence on business competitors, adulterous spouses, or, if you like, the neighbor two doors down who allows his dog to defecate on your lawn. In short, anyone pursuing any endeavor, professional or private, who could benefit from the clandestine gathering of information will benefit from this book.

Call it what you will: undercover work, spying, clandestine operations—creating the illusion that one is something other than what he actually is began with the birth of mankind. The Old Testament is full of examples, the first being in the third chapter of Genesis when Satan, masquerading as an angel in the form of a serpent, deceives Eve and convinces her to disobey God and eat from the Tree of Conscience. What follows reads like a classic police report for an investigation using informants. If you substitute an illegal substance such as cocaine for the Forbidden Fruit, you get a classic example of an investigator climbing the ladder of a drug empire, from a street dealer to the man at the top. God (the investigator) busts Adam (the illicit drug/fruit user), who doesn't hesitate to turn informant and give up Eve (both user and illegal distributor of the controlled/forbidden substance). Then Eve immediately "rolls over" (snitches) on Satan (the "Mr. Big" at the top of the whole illegal/forbidden operation).

Although the ancient Japanese ninja are more often pictured scaling walls to assassinate enemies with exotic weapons, they were skilled in undercover operations and used clandestine infiltration methods to get close to their victims. Agents of various ninja clans, such as Iga and Koga, passed themselves off as merchants, farmers, household servants, and sometimes even members of the samurai class. Working for whoever met their price (usually the samurai whose code of bushido precluded using the underhanded techniques the ninja employed), these silent warriors served as "rent-a-spys," who were not unlike today's hired security officers who pose as customers in order to catch shoplifters or dishonest employees.

History is full of examples in which clandestine operations were used for military and political purposes. Moses sent undercover men to infiltrate Jericho before the ancient Hebrews attacked the walls. In fact, in every war since, there is evidence that each side sent out agents to pose as the enemy in order to gather intelligence and carry out clandestine assassinations, steal documents, or commit sabotage. Kingdoms have been won and lost, monarchs have been assassinated, and the course of history has been altered by tongues that wagged in front of enemies posing as friends. In our own time, organizations like the Central Intelligence Agency (CIA), the Soviet State Security Committee (KGB), and the world's various military intelligence units have developed the art of role camouflage to near perfection.

On the home front, perceptive police administrators are aware that few criminals are stupid enough to perpetrate their crimes in the presence of law enforcement officials and have recognized the need for clandestine operatives disguised either as citizens or fellow criminals. The Drug Enforcement Administration (DEA), Bureau of Alcohol, Tobacco, and Firearms (BATF), Secret Service (SS), Federal Bureau of Investigation (FBI), and most state, county, and local agencies frequently use undercover men and women.

The key to successful undercover operations is informants. The development and use of informants will be discussed at length in Chapter 11, but for now the old street adage, "The man comes as a friend, with a friend," sums up the sentiment quite well. "Going in cold" or "winging it" (attempting to gain the confidence of a criminal or criminal group without a proper introduction by a member of that group) works only under the most unusual circumstances. In most cases, it should be avoided, as it is perhaps the easiest way to get "burned" or "blow the cover" you worked so hard to establish.

A second proverb of undercover work comes not from the bad guys but from the guys with the "beards," or disguises, themselves: Always have a story and a reason to be there. These are words the clandestine operative must live by. Developing this philosophy will reduce the number of impromptu explanations necessary to cover the inevitable contradictions that occur while an officer is undercover. A good story will protect the officer better than the best .45.

Although some federal agencies offer quality training to

members of local departments, most of this training focuses on the management of large operations. Very few hours are spent teaching actual undercover work itself, and training stops short of the detailed business of creating an alternate character, becoming that character for a specific length of time, and, perhaps most importantly, how to come out of that criminal persona when the operation is complete.

But that's okay. That is where *Going Undercover* begins.

Acknowledgments

Ed Hasbrook, Gary Campbell, Jim Cash, Ed Porter, Catherine Johnson, and Hale Photo—photography; Becky Cook, Jed Cook, Dee Cordry, Jim Keating, Norma Keating, Nancy Berland, Janet Runge, Johnna Runge, Kari Grant, Bob Howard, Danny Graham, Susie Pritchett, Connie Todd, Chad Brown, Hannah Saadah, Scott Walsh, Hubbard Taylor, Jim Hatfield, Tony Hatfield, Betty Powers, E.D. Howard, Ken Harrison, Mike Filson, Mary Howell, Pearl Stonebraker, Noah Callaway, Chauntel Booth, Brian Dowdy, Susan Martin, Nick Cole, Josh Smith, Jeremy Huntley, David Martin, Anna Maria Rodriguez, Chris Ladesau, Katherina Cahen, Cole Cofer, Earlene Cofer, Mark Willoughby, Cherlynn Bowlan, Alvin Williams, James Cookerly, Ray Furr, Gus Cook-Furr, Bari Cook, Tibbie Shades, Virginia Shades, Thomas Jerry Turpin, and Willie Scott—technical assistance.

A certain debt of gratitude is owed to every officer I've

ever worked with, as I learned something from each and every one of them. Special recognition, however, goes to DeWade Langley, Alvin Williams, and Larry "Leroy" Williams of the Tri-Agency Narcotics (TAN) unit. Thank you Jim Dempewolf, Russ Higby, and Jerry Harris—you know why. Thanks also to Ted Jones for covering my posterior more times than I can remember, Bill Addington for keeping me relatively sane, and Bob Burnett and Dennis McFadden for always being there. More appreciation goes to Sheriff Pat McFadden, who believed in Mark and me when others didn't, and who had the good sense to send us to Sid Cookerly for training. To Sid, too, who transforms the "exploring" life-style into an art form.

A Special Message to Women Undercover Officers

First, let me say that I admire the courage you display in working undercover. I am not certain I would be as courageous if I were a woman; not because women are less capable of undercover work, but because they have been led to believe they might be.

Unlike many areas of law enforcement, undercover work has never been closed to women. The fact is, women have been welcomed into the fold, encouraged, and even sought after. The reason is practical rather than political: most bad guys are just that—bad *guys*. And since most guys are heterosexual, they are drawn to women in a much different way than they are drawn to other men. A male criminal may consider a male undercover officer to be a fine person with whom to do business, drink beer, or play poker. But if he is heterosexual and the undercover officer is female, there will be one more aspect involved. To put it bluntly, he is very likely to view her as a possible sexual partner. This gives you an advantage over male officers. It also means that you not only have the potential to be as good undercover as men, you have the potential to be better.

If the best looking male undercover officer in the world asks a heterosexual male drug dealer to sell him illegal drugs, the drug dealer may say no. If a female officer asks the same drug dealer for the same dope, the answer may also be no, but he won't say no quite as quickly, and that little hesitation may eventually lead him to change his mind. This difference between men and women undercover officers, however, is a double-edged sword, bringing with it a frightening disadvantage: the risk of being raped. While men are not completely excluded from this terrifying possibility (remember that they often deal with ex-cons who hop on each other like rabbits), the threat is far greater to the woman officer. When you work undercover, you deal with the dregs of society, many of whose members think no more of taking you forcefully than they do of changing a flat tire on their stolen car. You are the only person who can make sure this does not happen.

The good news is that you are every bit as capable of preventing your rape, assault, or murder as your male colleagues are. Nothing can ensure that someone, male or female, will not get hurt undercover, but proper training with weapons and in unarmed self-defense can make you equal to men in that regard. Train harder, longer, and better, and you will become superior to them in these skills. About the only thing you cannot change is the physiological fact that the average man has more upper body strength than the average woman. This is, however, about as significant to the undercover female as the fact that you cannot write your name in the snow with urine or donate to a sperm bank. I have had to physically defend myself numerous times undercover, and I have yet to encounter a situation where the best defense was to bench press my attacker.

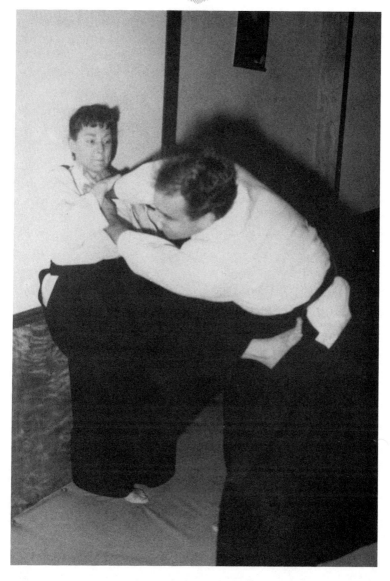

These female Jiyushinkai aikido practitioners (above and pages xiv and xv) are smaller and physically weaker than their opponents, but both are able to hold their own. Proper training in a self-defense-oriented combative art can render an attacker's advantages of strength and size useless. (Photos by Jim Cash)

The vast majority of information in *Going Undercover* applies equally to men and women. In the few cases where gender does make a difference, the differences are easy to spot. I have chosen to use the masculine viewpoint for the simple reason that constantly saying "he or

she" and "him and her" makes for cumbersome writing that detracts from the text, and resorting to such tricks as substituting "they" for he or she is grammatically incorrect—a correctness on which I put far more importance than the political variety.

In closing, I have worked with many women in an undercover capacity over the years and found them to be no different from men in one respect: some were excellent officers, others were not. Only you can decide which category you will fall into. I wish you luck.

Introduction

Under specific and controlled circumstances, almost anyone is capable of working undercover. Some officers, however, shun such assignments, while others are drawn to the challenge like addicts to a crack house. The question that inevitably arises from law enforcement officers who cannot conceive of masquerading as criminals is, "What kind of idiot would even want to?"

This is a reasonable question. The undercover officer must live in a sewer without getting dirty himself. He must reside in a world infected with murderers, thieves, drug pushers, addicts, pimps, and whores. He must brush shoulders with human beings (or at least two-legged animals posing as humans) who think no more of killing someone than they do of squashing a bug with their shoe. It is a world of corruption, debauchery, and downright evil. Right and wrong are reversed. The honest, hardworking individual is considered to be a fool, and the best liars, thieves, and killers are respected. So who willingly enters this world? To help answer that question, police officers must be divided into two distinct personality types: Explorers and Homesteaders. But before I continue, a short explanation of these labels is necessary.

America was settled in the last century by two different types of individuals. The explorers came first, blazing new trails in unmapped and mysterious lands. Being a wild, self-sufficient lot, they picked fruit and vegetables, gathered wild grains, and hunted for food as they went. They risked their fortunes and their lives simply to see what no white European had seen before.

In doing so, they charted the way for the homesteaders. The explorers didn't stay anywhere long enough to establish roots, but when the homesteaders came, they planted crops and built houses, churches, and schools. They set up governments and, in general, did their best to organize and civilize the untamed lands. Their goal was to create a secure and stable environment, which was exactly what the explorers were trying to escape. Explorers did not need, want, or understand that degree of organization, security, or stability.

Today's Americans are the descendants of these explorers and homesteaders. You can see the "Homesteader" personality in the corporate executive and the "Explorer" in the salesmen who work for him. The chairman of a university music department may be a Homesteader, but you can bet your bottom dollar that the musicians are Explorers. The doctor in charge of a hospital's administration is undoubtedly a Homesteader, but the surgeon who uses a steak knife to perform an impromptu tracheotomy on a choking man is an Explorer. Police officers are not excepted from these designations.

To divide all police officers or people in any other group into two tidy little personality categories is, of course, an oversimplification of gross proportions. Most officers possess at least some traits from both personality types. If this were not the case, the Explorer would be incapable of writing an intelligent report, and the Homesteader would have never chosen a career in police work to begin with. Yet most officers exhibit either more Homesteader or more Explorer characteristics. Looking at extreme examples from both groups is helpful to discern what type of individual makes a good undercover officer.

As a rule, the Homesteaders who are found in any police organization do not like change. They are intent on maintaining the status quo or changing it slowly through conventional means. They believe that things are done a certain way because years of trial and error have proven those policies to be effective. Homesteaders are quite content to plod along at "dull-but-necessary" routine work, if that's what it takes to get the job done. (You plant the corn, then you harvest the corn, then you plant the corn again . . .) Homesteaders have a clear view of long-range goals, and this pushes them forward, even when short-term success is not evident. They are detail-oriented and believe strongly in team effort: everyone must do their part for the good of the whole. (Japanese Homesteaders made great kamikaze pilots in World War II.) Homesteaders do not "create waves" in their departments. On the contrary, they are always the first to be promoted. They believe strongly in the chain of command and respecting their superiors, and they expect their subordinates to have the same beliefs and respect for them. Many have a tendency to "suck up and spit down." Homesteaders tend to be overly conservative; send one to Las Vegas with $5,000 and he'll stick it in the bank and collect interest until it's time for his flight home.

Explorers are the antithesis of Homesteaders because they thrive on change. To the Explorer, change is not threatening—stagnation is. The Explorer thrives on the security of insecurity—the knowledge that things are "about to break." They suspect that most departmental policy was written to personally benefit whoever wrote it and to make their job harder. Want to punish an Explorer? It's easy. Just put him in charge of the monthly uniform crime reports, or some other repetitive task that requires the same work day after day, week after week, year after year. The Explorer finds boredom to be the most torturous of all mental states and would rather be scared out of his underwear than sitting around twiddling his thumbs.

The Explorer has fears, but they are very different from the fears that plague the Homesteader. A Homesteader involved in a shooting fears being shot. An Explorer involved in the same shooting will worry more about the shame he will feel if he empties his gun at the assailant and all of his rounds miss. What is the Explorer's most secret fear? That he will be promoted and turn into a Homesteader.

The Explorer, you see, doesn't want to keep planting and harvesting the corn. It might be fun to plant it once—he's never done that before—but afterwards he'd rather leave the harvest to a Homesteader while he went off in search of new fields. Explorers need high levels of excitement, change, and short-term reinforcement. They are distracted from tedious pursuits easier than their Homesteader brothers but are far more capable of handling the unexpected. When an Explorer finds his life going too smoothly (read that monotonously), he often complicates it, consciously or unconsciously. Send an Explorer on the same trip to Las Vegas and when he gets back he'll either be broke or a millionaire.

Whether you're a police officer or not, I suspect you've already determined which of these groups you fall into. You've also probably thought of a few irritating, often maddening people you know who fall into the opposite category. If you're a Homesteader, you find the Explorers you know to be disorganized, impulsive, and even childish. They have no respect for time (or much of anything else, for that matter), they're often ill-mannered, and they exhibit a distinct inability to follow orders. And they just flat daydream too damn much, don't they?

If you're an Explorer, however, you view your traits as assets rather than liabilities. The truth is, you feel the Homesteaders are so busy organizing things that they never get around to doing anything. What they view as impulsiveness, you see as the ability to change—to react and handle the unforeseen events life throws in your path.

You may look disorganized, but you aren't—you know the exact location of every warrant, investigative report, and intelligence file in that pile of paper that rises from the top of your desk to the ceiling. It's not that you can't follow orders, it's just that you won't follow some of the stupid orders the Homesteaders hand out. (It's been so long since those Homesteaders were on the streets that they've forgotten what's going on out there.) Okay, you'll concede that maybe you daydream some, but that's only because you're bored to tears with superfluous paperwork. Ill-mannered? Who has time for manners? And they're dead wrong when they call you insubordinate and disrespectful. It's just that you wouldn't be able to look at your face when you shaved if you brownnosed the brass all day like the Homesteaders.

As you might have already guessed, when Homesteaders and Explorers come together, conflict is inevitable, and that conflict has been a theme for novels, films, and television programs ever since those mediums of entertainment came into existence. For example, Homesteader Roger Murtaugh (Danny Glover) has a hard time understanding Explorer Martin Riggs (Mel Gibson) in the first *Lethal Weapon* movie, and when Glover begins to exhibit his own Explorer tendencies in the sequels, the director pulls in a Homesteader captain to scream his frustration and provide the essential conflict. Ian Fleming's Homesteading M pulls his hair out by the roots every time one of Explorer 007's sexual indiscretions threatens to embarrass the Queen, and Homesteader cops and politicians have tried to block Explorer Mike Hammer's unorthodox methods of investigation in print and on screen since Mickey Spillane gave birth to Hammer.

By now, it should come as no surprise that, while there are exceptions, the vast majority of successful undercover officers are Explorers. And the answer to the question, "Why do they willingly enter the seedy, disgusting, violent, and dangerous world of criminals?" should be equally clear: to avoid boredom. Even the challenges of uniform patrol or straight investigation eventually become monotonous to the Explorer. He needs more to satisfy his deep-seated hunger for adventure.

If it sounds like I'm up on Explorers and down on Homesteaders, I can't help it; I'm an Explorer myself, and I exhibit all of the strengths and weaknesses typical of that group. When I go to a Dirty Harry movie, I identify with Harry when the captain chews him out. I also wonder if some of the Homesteader supervisors I've had over the years are sitting in the audience saying to themselves, "Ream his butt out good, Captain. Harry was way out of line violating departmental policy like that."

In truth, though, it takes both Homesteaders and Explorers to make the world turn, and it takes both to make a police agency function properly. (You'll never know how much it hurt to say that, but it's true.) If there were no Homesteaders, there would be little organization, and the necessary documentation would never get done. But if there were no Explorers, there would be nothing to document. When Homesteaders and Explorers understand their limitations and acknowledge the strengths possessed by their opposites, they work well together, with each side taking up the slack left by the other group. This seems fairly complex, but in reality it is very simple.

These are all things to ponder if you're considering undercover work, but, in short, if your heart draws you toward it, and you get an adrenaline rush just thinking about it, chances are you'll make a good undercover officer. But if you don't jump at the idea, you need time to think about it, or you are only considering undercover work because it might be good to have in your file come promotion time, you're probably better off taking another route within the department.

I'll be talking to Explorers from now on, and I'll probably take a lot of cheap shots at the Homesteaders along the way. But don't worry, Homesteaders, you guys are still way ahead in the ongoing war. You always keep your noses clean, and you get the promotions, which means we Explorers have to take a lot of crap from you at work.

PART 1

GETTING SET UP

CHAPTER 1

Creating an Undercover Identity

There's far more to creating an undercover identity than simply picking out a new name. You are about to give birth to a different person, and you must be able to create the illusion of being that person under varying degrees of scrutiny. Therefore, that person must be every bit as deep, well-rounded, and complex as a real human being.

YOUR UNDERCOVER NAME

The name is the logical place to begin. Except under extremely special circumstances, such as posing as a dishonest cop, you are not going to use your real name. (Such opportunities occasionally arise but are actually more like semi-undercover assignments.) There are obvious reasons for changing your name, one being so the bad guys have to look farther than the phone book to find you after they've bonded out. But there are much deeper reasons than that.

Changing Your Last Name

At the very least, your last name must be changed. This is particularly important if you work in a small- to medium-sized town, but it should also be done if you work in a major city, even if your assignment is 2,000 miles from home. Criminals get around like anybody else, often more. Johnny Jones, the Dallas coke dealer your informant is about to introduce to you, might turn out to be the same Johnny Jones you arrested for public drunkenness six years ago when you were a Kansas City patrolman. Unless there was something unique about Johnny's case, you aren't likely to remember a public drunkenness arrest. To Johnny, however, the experience held far more significance.

Let's look at some situations that may exist. Unbeknownst to you, the biggest, meanest resident in the county jail fell in love with Johnny. When he was through, he decided it wasn't love after all, and passed Johnny around to his friends. Johnny had quite a night. And who does he blame? You. He was drunk when you arrested him and doesn't have a great recollection of your face, but for the last six years he's hated it no matter what it looks like. Then your informant introduces you to Johnny. Sure, you look different from how you looked six years ago . . . but there's something familiar about you. At the very least, Johnny knows he's met you somewhere before. At this point you can say, "Yeah, you look familiar too. I wonder where we met?" and it'll probably drop at that.

But suppose you're going by your real name, and suppose it's Richard Miller. Johnny is more likely to remember the name Richard Miller than he is your face since by the time the public defender had given him his copy of the paperwork, he'd been raped into sobriety. Now here you come with a face that looks familiar, and when you shake Johnny's hand and say, "Hi, I'm Rich Miller," he's got a second point of reference that suddenly connects what would have otherwise been an obscure and unrelated memory. Bang! You're dead, Richard, and your wife is suing the insurance company because they're trying to weasel out of paying off.

Changing Your First Name

All of the experts I know agree about changing the last name, but there are two schools of thought regarding undercover first names. The first school maintains that you should use your real first name, because under the pressure of an undercover assignment, you, your partner, or your informant may forget and use it anyway. Many knowledgeable and well-respected professionals, among them members of the DEA, subscribe to this theory. You should consider it.

The second philosophy, to which I subscribe, is to change the first name as well as the last. Then you do the proper "homework" to ensure that the new appellation comes as naturally to you, and anyone else with whom you will be undercover, as your old one.

It seems logical to me that the "Johnny Jones syndrome" could plague you almost as easily by a criminal remembering your first name as your last. In fact, there's an important downside to using either of your real names. What will you do if you're undercover and you accidentally run into someone who has met you in real life, and you are using your real name? Don't tell me it's unlikely to happen. I already know that. I also know that the long shot sometimes isn't so long—it's happened . . . to me.

I was standing on the corner of NE 23rd Street and Broadway in Oklahoma City one summer afternoon several years ago, calmly setting up a heroin buy with a well-known smack dealer I'd been working on for weeks. Everything was going well; he trusted me, and we were about to shake hands and go our separate ways until that evening when the deal would go down. All of a sudden, I heard a voice at my side say, "Jerry! Jerry VanCook?" I was in my undercover role, and I didn't turn. A moment later, I heard, "Jerry VanCook?" again. That time the voice was obviously right next to me, and there was no doubt that it was directed at me. I turned to see the smiling face of the kid brother of an old friend from my hometown a hundred miles away.

"Are you talking to me?" I asked in the surliest voice I could muster.

"Well . . . yeah . . . Jerry . . . ?"

"No, I'm not Jerry, fuckhead," I said. "And I'm busy, so get your ass away from me before I peel it up over your ears." (I hope foul language doesn't offend you. The bad guys at the lower end of the food chain use it a lot, and if you want to appear to be a bad guy, you'd better get used to using it too.)

"Gee . . . I'm sorry," the kid said. "You look just like this friend of my brother's . . ." His voice trailed off.

I glowered at him, silently praying he'd leave before he finished the sentence, ". . . a friend of my brother's who's a cop." I guess he decided I wasn't the type to appreciate police officers as family friends, and he turned on his heels and beat it down the street.

The heroin dealer knew me as Mickey. He bought my act, and we had a few laughs about the "stupid son of a bitch." The deal went down that night, and, as far as I know, the dealer is still in the penitentiary. I was lucky, but I wonder how lucky I'd have been if I was going by Jerry. It's one thing to look like someone else, but it's entirely another to resemble someone who has the same name. A coincidence like that is just too great to overlook. Things could have gotten ugly, and at the very least, a deal that had taken weeks to set up could have gone right down the tubes.

(By the way, I bumped into the same kid again about three months later, and he told me about meeting my evil twin. I didn't have the heart to set him straight.)

Choosing an Appropriate Undercover Name

So, do you still want to play the game? Good. Then it's time to decide what your undercover name will be. Mike Hammer? Mack Bolan? Johnny Danger? How about Chuck Norris, or Arnold Schwarzenegger, or Sylvester Stallone? Believe it or not, I've known undercover officers who went by names almost this ridiculous.

I'm going to let you in on a little secret that all undercover officers know but don't like to talk about. The fact is that in the back of our brains, hearts, and souls but veiled on the surface as well as we can veil it, we all think we're pretty neat. We have fantasies that we're at least a little bit like James Bond, or Charles Bronson, or Clint Eastwood. Well, that's okay; undercover officers are creative people, or they wouldn't have gotten into this area of law enforcement to begin with. But this type of thinking has got to be kept in perspective. So, while you're telling yourself that if you were 4 inches taller, 20 pounds lighter, and had blond hair, you'd look just like Dolph Lundgren, try to keep the other foot in the real world.

Like every other part of your undercover persona, the name you choose should fit the character you are portraying. People conjure up images from a name. If you don't believe this, try picturing the person who belongs to this name: Reginald Balforth Remington, III. Now, does the same picture pop into your head when I say Shorty Watson or Gus Webster? Fiction writers spend many hours coming up with appropriate names for their characters. You should do no less. If the name a writer settles on doesn't fit his character, his novel flops at the bookstore. If the name you choose doesn't fit your undercover character, you will flop on the street. (Yes, there's a double meaning there.)

YOUR FICTIONAL BIOGRAPHY

To portray your character convincingly you must know him well, and writing a detailed biography is the only way I have ever found to accomplish that. Start with the birth of your undercover character and bring him up to the age he is now. Include every detail of his life that you can think of to make him a well-rounded, deep, real human being. Don't worry about the quality of your writing. Feel free to go off on tangents and "rabbit chases" if you wish. The idea is to become intimately familiar with your character, not win the Pulitzer Prize for literature.

The first undercover identity I ever created was Mickey

Jordan. "Mick" was born in Ozark, Missouri, a little town about eight miles south of Springfield and my college roommate's hometown. I'd spent enough time there to know the area quite well, and after writing what turned out to be a 300-page biography of Mick's life, I knew him, too. I knew what kind of grades he'd made in high school, that he'd played defensive tackle on the high school football team, and that he'd been a drummer in a highly unsuccessful rock-and-roll band that did little more than practice in the lead guitar player's garage and disrupt the neighborhood every Sunday

Writing a detailed biography of your newly created identity, though a lengthy process, is time well spent. It instills the character in your subconscious mind and helps you provide believable answers to many of the questions the bad guys will ask. (Photo by Edward Hasbrook)

afternoon. More importantly, I knew how to talk about being a defensive tackle and a bad drummer, since Jerry VanCook had done these things as well as Mickey Jordan.

Do you see what I'm driving at here? When you create a new character, you must draw from your own experiences in order to make that character believable. Never, ever profess to know something you are not informed about. For instance, if you tell someone that you went to the University of Central Oklahoma (UCO) and majored in anthropology, sooner or later you'll meet someone who really did go to school there and knows that UCO doesn't have an anthropology department. Tell someone you play rhythm guitar and watch how quickly you find out that the guy not only has his own band, but his rhythm guitar player just died of alcohol/barbiturate poisoning, and he desperately needs somebody to fill in at a gig that night.

For the most part, Mickey Jordan was a reasonably intelligent guy who hung out in seedy places and fraternized with blue-collar criminals. But he knew how to knot a necktie when it came time to clean up his act, too. Old Mick might be a drug dealer one day, a gun runner the next, and a burglar the day after that, but he had the most fun when he got to play hit man. He was a pretty friendly guy, but there was also an underlying ambience of violence surrounding him. Mick had been arrested for everything from possession of marijuana to manslaughter. He'd done a little county jail time but had no felony convictions. The reason for this was twofold: first, the fact that he'd always beaten the rap insinuated that Mick had a certain animal intelligence that I wanted him to possess. Second, and more importantly, I didn't know anything about penitentiaries at the time.

Picture this scene: you're undercover, sitting in Frank Baker's living room, waiting for his partner to deliver a load of heroin so you can make your first buy. You were introduced to Frank by an informant, and everything's going well. You're killing time until the smack gets there, and Frank asks you if you've ever done any time.

"Yeah," you say. "Did two years at Big Mac (the Oklahoma State Penitentiary at McAlester)."

"No shit?" Frank says. "When?"

"Got out last July." You're beginning to get a little uneasy, because you suddenly realize that the only thing you know about Big Mac is what you used to see when you delivered prisoners there as a deputy sheriff.

Some criminals have access to the National Crime Information Center (NCIC) through friends, relatives, or dirty cops. Having a criminal record under your undercover identity can mean the difference between a successful portrayal of your role and disaster. (Photo by Edward Hasbrook)

"Well I'll be damned," Frank says. "You must have known an old buddy of mine, Butch Johnson."

Okay, the moment of truth is nearing. Was Butch Johnson really there when you were supposed to be, or is Frank testing you? For that matter, does a real Butch Johnson even exist?

Playing it safe, you say, "Hell, don't remember him. But that's a big place."

Frank nods. "Yeah, that's what Butch said."

You breathe a sigh of relief, but it's short-lived.

"Butch was on cell block three. Where were you?" Frank asks casually.

Here it is, boys and girls, the moment of truth. You've backed yourself in a corner, and all you can hope for is that God hears the prayers racing through your brain. You figure if there's a cell block three, there has to be a one and two as well. "Two," you finally say.

Frank smiles. "I was at Mac last year myself," he says. "Block two was still being reconstructed after the fire, and nobody was on it."

Whoops. Hope your wife has a good attorney, because I see her in line at the insurance company again.

THE UNDERCOVER BILLFOLD

After you choose your undercover name and write your character's fictional biography, it's time to put together an undercover billfold. A good way to get started is to pull out your own wallet and see what you have in it, then start duplicating the items under your new name. You'll need a driver's license, Social Security card, and credit cards. These can be obtained legally through your department, regardless of what that Homesteader supervisor who's been permanently epoxied to his desk tells you. Keep after him to get it done.

Your undercover billfold should include such major pieces of identification as a driver's license, but don't forget the little things that add credence to your identity, such as ticket stubs, receipts, etc. (Photo by Edward Hasbrook)

You may never need them—but if you do, you'll need them bad, and you'll need them right away. Until you obtain these items, carry no identification on you whatsoever.

To these basic documents you should add all of the little "frills" that make a wallet look believable. Crumpled receipts, pawn tickets, and phone numbers written on the back of matchbook covers all lend authenticity to your identity. If you carry photographs, they should not be of real family members, of course, and if you can obtain pictures from a friend halfway across the country, so much the better. Make sure that every item is in keeping with the personality your character has. Mickey Jordan, for instance, did not have a Niemann-Marcus credit card and would not have been caught dead carrying opera ticket stubs.

UNDERCOVER OCCUPATIONS

Finally, you need to create both legal and illegal occupations for your character. Again, they must be chosen from areas you know well. Since I had been a karate teacher before entering law enforcement, Mickey Jordan was a martial arts instructor who was usually in town looking for a site to open a dojo. From time to time, I would meet other black belts undercover, and the fact that I could speak with authority on the subject helped confirm the illusion I was creating. (It also prompted a challenge once that ended in a knock-down-drag-out fight, but what the hell, everything has its downside, right?) My proposed karate school was always planned as a front for Mickey's other dealings, which included fencing stolen goods, burglary, drugs, or whatever else fit the specific assignment. The dojo could just have easily been a plumbing shop, music store, quick lube/oil change franchise, or anything else. Mickey might have been looking for a job as a bricklayer, a cook at McDonald's, or a CPA, depending upon the type of criminals with whom he was associating.

CHAPTER 2

Creating an Alternate Personality

Your undercover identity is your name and your background, or, as Sergeant Friday used to say, "Just the facts, ma'am." Your undercover personality determines how that identity acts within and responds to its environment.

Novelists claim that there is a little bit of themselves in every character they create. Actors draw from their own experiences in order to convincingly portray specific roles. As an undercover operative, you are both writer and actor with one very important difference: if a writer fails to convince his readers that his characters are believable, people don't buy his books; if an actor turns in a less-than-acceptable performance, no one goes to his movies; but if you, as an undercover officer, do either of these things, the bad guys will kill you.

FITTING IN

How you act undercover depends upon the type of criminals you are dealing with. You must try to fit in and create the illusion that you are one of them. This means looking, acting, dressing, speaking, and even thinking the way they do. If you find yourself investigating white collar crime and are surrounded by Ivy League professionals who sue people when they get mad instead of hitting them, it would be foolish to look, dress, or act like Randall "Tex" Cobb in the movie *Raising Arizona*. On the other hand, if you're riding with outlaw bikers or hanging out with a gang of skinheads, you'd better be prepared to get down in the trenches and be as tough as these people are.

Anyone who doesn't believe that America has a class system hasn't been paying attention. America may not have specific names or titles for royalty, peasants, and the landed gentry, but they are present nonetheless. In his excellent, and often hilarious, book *Class* (New York: Ballantine Books, 1983), Paul Fussell divides our populace not into the three to five classes that are generally accepted but into a caste system that includes 12 distinct levels. As an undercover officer, you must be able to create the illusion that you belong to any one of these classes. Consider picking up a copy of Fussell's book. It's an excellent resource to help you determine when to order a domestic beer and when a "martoonie" (shaken, not stirred) is more appropriate.

READING PEOPLE

A rule of thumb in undercover work is, the further you drop into the dregs of society, the more dangerous your job becomes. In general, the more money people are making at their criminal endeavors, the less likely they are to be violent—directly, at least. In other words, the man at the top may have people working for him who break arms and legs, but he, in creating his own illusion of respectability, usually doesn't get his own hands dirty. (But, be prepared for exceptions to this rule.)

A good undercover officer develops an ability to read the people with whom he associates to determine their potential for violence. A great undercover officer not only does this but never forgets that he might underestimate that potential. If you stay in the business long enough, you will eventually see someone you thought of as a mouse suddenly turn into a lion.

TEMPERAMENT AND DEMEANOR

Because violence is most likely to occur when you are dealing with criminals on the lower end of the social scale (but beware the exception to this rule), there is a fine line you must walk when masquerading as a "lowlife." Somehow, as Mickey Jordan was usually able to do, you must make it known that you are capable of killing or beating the hell out of anybody who gets in your way. But you must do this in a way that is not a direct challenge. (Sound familiar? "The best defense is a good offense," "peace through superior firepower", "walk softly and carry a big stick," and all that.) Never back anyone into a corner where their honor is at stake, especially in front of their friends, associates, or, in particular, their girlfriend or wife.

How is this accomplished? Primarily through demeanor, and that is something that takes time and work. For a start, try to remember a movie you've seen in which an actor like Clint Eastwood or Charles Bronson successfully pulled it off. They each have a look in their eyes that sends chills down the bad guys' spines.

"But they're actors, and that's the movies," I can hear some of you say. "This is real life."

That's true, but keep in mind that you are an actor, too. And people are more influenced by the entertainment world than they'd like to admit. When a criminal goes to the theater and watches Arnold Schwarzenegger's facial expressions and body language, he remembers those mannerisms at a subconscious level. He associates the lowering of an eyebrow with bad guys getting the hell beat out of them, and when he hears Arnold say, "I'll be back," he knows the hero will be shooting when he returns. Even though some criminals have dealt with real cops since their first juvenile bust, they have still seen more cops on TV and in the movies, and the differences they perceive between Hollywood and real life are not as distinct as one might like to think. Cops are susceptible to this as well. (How many detectives do you know who wore horizontal shoulder holsters before the airing of *Miami Vice*?)

But the movies are just the beginning—a place to start—in developing your own techniques. Watch what the tough guys do on screen, then translate what you see to real life as it fits your undercover personality and each undercover situation. Then, as with every aspect of undercover work, do not count on these techniques entirely.

Certain looks, movements, and gestures can indicate to the bad guys that you will hurt them if it becomes necessary. But because these threats are made abstractly and are never verbalized, the bad guys are not directly challenged and have no need to defend their honor. But each bad guy has a unique personality, and he interprets what he sees a little differently from anyone else. Therefore, the short stare you are hoping will say, "I don't particularly want to fight, but I will if I have to," may be perceived as, "I think I'll just kill you, rob you, and maybe rape your girlfriend, sister, and mother while I'm at it."

Sometimes, showing your associates that you may be even a little bit crazier than they are is effective. An easygoing personality that is punctuated occasionally by driving your fist through the wallboard for some minor irritation is helpful. (Try to avoid the studs—they're usually 16 inches apart and hurt like hell when you hit them.) A brief "fire in the eyes" look that lasts only a few seconds and then disappears to become a less-than-sincere smile can convey the same thing in some situations. Use your imagination. God gave you one when he made you an Explorer.

There are also some two-man techniques for doing this

that can be effective if you are undercover with a partner or informant. One of the best I ever used was one that my partner, Mark, and I worked out. Bear in mind that I am a little under 6 feet tall, was doing a lot of power-lifting during my undercover days, weighed about 250 pounds, and have a face that I'm pretty sure my mother loved anyway. Mark, on the other hand, was about 5 feet 6 inches tall and would have been hard pressed to tip the scales at 160 pounds. When we felt a situation warranted it, I'd begin a gradual escalation of surliness that would climax with the appearance that I was about to really crack and turn the place into firewood. Then, Mark would walk over to me, reach up, and slap me across the face.

"I've had all the crap out of you I'm gonna put up with tonight," he'd say, at which point I'd begin apologizing profusely.

No one ever said anything when we did this number, but you could see what they were thinking written across their faces: "If the big guy is afraid of the little guy . . . God help us . . . what does the little guy do when he's mad?"

Remember that although you are a cop, you are an actor as well. You must be creative in developing your own subtle (or not-so-subtle, as in the case above, but still nonthreatening) ways of instilling in the minds of the bad guys the illusions you want them to have.

DRESS

How you dress speaks volumes about your character and must always fit the situation and the criminals you have targeted. If you are meeting with the president of a toxic waste disposal company to discuss how to illegally dump the U.S. Army's toxic waste, you are not going to enter the boardroom wearing a leather motorcycle jacket, ripped blue jeans covered with axle grease, and knee-high combat boots. But if you're going to a tavern called Miss Fit's where the local motorcycle scum go to drink, fight, sell methamphetamine, and engage in their usual debauchery, this outfit *might* be perfect.

Did you notice the emphasis on the word might? That's because it might *not* be perfect, too. Criminals are as style conscious as anyone else, and the "little things" you wear can be a dead giveaway that you are not actually what you appear to be. Every criminal faction has its own unofficial dress code, and while there is usually room for variety within those standards, if you step too far over the line you will be labeled an imposter. For instance, in the boardroom this year, "rep" ties may be out of fashion and paisley may be in. In Miss Fit's, the newest craze may be black studded cowboy boots instead of the more traditional round-toed motorcycle footwear.

Do your homework ahead of time. Know exactly what you should or shouldn't wear, depending upon who you're dealing with. While little mistakes like last year's boots or tie are not likely to be significant by themselves, they can instigate enough suspicion to cause a bad guy to look for other discrepancies. If this happens, you will learn the hard way that Kurt Lewin's theory about synergy also applies to undercover work: the whole is greater than the sum of the parts.

STAYING IN CHARACTER

As long as I'm using mathematical metaphors, here's another: every aspect of your undercover identity and personality must add up to a believable character. Like an actor, you must stay in character while on an undercover assignment regardless of what happens or how long the assignment lasts. This is not as hard as it sounds, since the vast majority of undercover work is short-term. What is usually referred to as "deep cover" (setting up and living with the bad guys) is quite rare and financially not feasible for most departments, agencies, or bureaus.

Your undercover personality, by and large, will not

Your undercover character must be flexible enough to tackle a wide variety of roles. (See photos on page 26 and 27 also.) He may be called upon to sip martinis with the chairman of the board at lunch and down long necks in a redneck honky-tonk bar later that night. (Photo by Gary Campbell)

(Photo by Edward Hasbrook)

need to be much different from your real one. If you are
quiet by nature, fine. So are a lot of drug dealers, thieves,

(Photo by Catherine Johnson)

and murderers. If you are gregarious, that works too and can be advantageous in working your way into the confidence of the bad guys. (Just don't let your mouth overload your derriere, as the saying goes.)

FLEXIBILITY

Perhaps the greatest distinction between your undercover identity and undercover personality is that the identity remains the same, while the personality must be flexible enough to fit into whatever environment you enter. For example, the Mickey Jordan who enters a boardroom will more than likely go by the full name on his undercover driver's license: Michael J. Jordan. He will also laugh good-naturedly at all the jokes he hears about being a tall, black basketball player who didn't quite make it in baseball. Then old Mick might put on a dirty cap advertising an oil field drilling company in order to buy stolen drill bits, and if he does, the twang in his speech will indicate that he was born in southeast Oklahoma, not Ozark, Missouri. If Mickey Jordan is a seedy strip-club owner who deals dope out of the back door, he may show up with perfectly styled hair, enough gold on his throat and fingers to make Mr. T jealous, and a manner of speech and cocky attitude appropriate to this type of individual. (If you don't know any greasy night-club owners who you can use as models, just think of some of the defense attorneys you've dealt with.)

CHARACTER TYPES

You are limited only by your imagination when it comes to the different personalities you can take on undercover, and each officer must create a character, or characters, that fit his basic personality as well as the situation. It is beneficial, however, to explore a few of the standard "types" that have proven to be effective over the years, since, with a few modifications to make them fit specific circumstances, they are useful.

The following four basic characters should help launch you on the road to creating your own unique undercover personality. There are countless other character types as well as limitless combinations. With experience, you will create a set of very unique personalities that you can step into and out of as circumstances demand.

The Tough-Guy Career Criminal

This was Mickey Jordan's forte. Usually, this guy has a high school education or less. He probably works off and on in a legitimate trade of some type but relies on small- to medium-sized criminal endeavors to supplement his income. He's probably dabbled in a lot of different areas, like burglary, drug dealing, and robbery. He's an opportunist who is flexible enough to take advantage of whatever illegal opportunities present themselves. He will almost always have an arrest record, unless he's just graduated from juvenile delinquent to full-fledged criminal. He is street smart, tough, and has a tough attitude toward life. He knows, and accepts, that at least part of his life is going to be spent behind bars—it's just a professional hazard. The strength of this character is his bad-ass attitude, which prevents him from being challenged very often. But this attitude can be his weakness also, because sooner or later a stranger will ride into Dodge City wanting to prove he's the faster gun.

Good Times Charlie

This character was especially successful back in the "hippie" days when there was an illusion of love circulating throughout the drug culture. (Most flower-children dope dealers are now dead at the hands of other drug dealers who didn't take that love stuff quite as seriously.) The Good Times Charlie character wants to have a good time at the party of life. He isn't particularly ambitious but may get into a low-risk criminal endeavor if it promises enough money for him to keep getting stoned. The strengths of this character are that he's nonthreatening to other criminals and often appears too goofy to be a cop. But Charlie's apparent passivity makes him a likely target for a rip-off, and in drug cases he comes off as a user rather than a dealer.

My partner, Mark, developed this character to an art. But remember that Mark could instantly change into the other character who liked to play "slap the big guy." Unless you are equally skilled, you may find yourself backed into a corner where you look real bad if you don't fire up a little crystal meth with the big boys.

The Burned-Out Hippie

This character comes in handy for those of us whose beards have turned gray, and it leaves a fairly wide range for covering the little discrepancies that inevitably come up undercover. Let's face it, all that acid back in the 1960s and 1970s took its toll, and that old fart in the bell-bottoms and platform shoes can't be expected to make sense all the time. But the burned-out hippie has some of the same problems as Good Times Charlie, and what's left of your Grateful Dead haircut may spell V-I-C-T-I-M to a younger criminal who was raised on a diet of heavy metal or hate rock.

The White-Collar Con Man

This is the guy I mentioned earlier who's helping the president of the toxic waste disposal company decide how to cut corners with the Environmental Protection Agency. This character is also the type who could figure out how to sell the government $5,000 toilet seats. This is an exceptionally good role for those rare individuals who are Explorers, but who also possess a lot of the better Homesteader characteristics. This is also the character most suited to Homesteaders who find themselves undercover. I once helped train and then worked with a young man who had a master of arts (MA) degree in accounting. He was pretty much a one-trick pony when it came to undercover work, but he did an excellent job as long as he stayed in this role.

When playing the white-collar con man, there is usually (don't ever forget what that word means) less chance of winding up with a bullet or blade in your chest than when you're dealing with bad guys who are farther down on the evolutionary chart. The guys in the ties are every bit as dangerous as the scum on the street, but instead of fighting with knives and guns, they use paper, computers, and brains. This means that there is always a greater opportunity to fall into some of the legal and political traps that will be discussed in Part 5.

ACTING

Remember that you are essentially an actor, but instead of having a complete script from which to work, you have only a general scenario of the story. You are the leading man, and you know who some of the other characters will be, but you must create your own dialogue and stage directions to fit the plot as it unfolds. There is one major difference, however, between doing Shakespeare in the park and working undercover: the audience that doesn't find your portrayal of Othello convincing may show their disapproval by throwing tomatoes at the stage—the bad guys you haven't convinced tend to throw bullets.

CHAPTER 3

Personal Transportation

Most major cities in the United States provide public transportation, and if you are working undercover where a subway or bus system is available, you may want to take advantage of it. Public transportation is about as anonymous as you can get, and a few stops or a roundabout course that leads toward a drug deal should enable you to determine whether or not the bad guys are running countersurveillance, which is becoming more common these days. (A few years ago, a bust at the home of a drug dealer by the Oklahoma City Police Department [OCPD] revealed some rather startling evidence: the dealer had intelligence files that included not only descriptions of vehicles used by the Oklahoma Bureau of Narcotics and Dangerous Drugs [OBNDD] but accurate names and descriptions of the agents themselves. Having secured the proper crystals to monitor OBNDD's radio frequency, he simply sat home, listened to his police scanner, and then sent his flunkies out to gather intelligence when radio traffic told him where various agents

While budget and other considerations often make obtaining the perfect vehicle impossible, do everything you can to ensure that your wheels fit the rest of your undercover persona. A good story should cover any discrepancies. (Photos by Edward Hasbrook)

were meeting for coffee or lunch. What is the lesson to be learned here? Never underestimate your enemy.)

For the most part, you will need your own "wheels." Your vehicle is more than just a way of getting from point A to point B; to many people, including criminals, it is a signature, and it can be a way for people to identify you even quicker than by seeing your face. Most people tend to subconsciously stereotype others by what they drive. For example, a new Mercedes means success, a 10-year-old Ford LTD covered with spots of gray primer paint spells failure, older men and women prefer Lincolns and Cadillacs, and a BMW means you're a yuppie. (Just don't forget to call it a "Beamer.") As with every other aspect of the illusion you create, your chosen means of transportation should fit your overall image. This is often more easily said than done.

OBTAINING UNDERCOVER VEHICLES

If the agency you work for is of any significant size, chances are it already has one or more undercover vehicles that were either purchased, seized, or donated. Each method of obtaining wheels has advantages and disadvantages for the undercover operative. If the budget permits, buying vehicles is preferable. This cuts down on the chances that the bad guys will recognize it if it was seized. For instance, the Chrysler New Yorker you're driving may be recognized as the one Tony McGillicutty used to own before he got caught with 10 kilos of hash in the trunk. This doesn't mean that seized vehicles have no place; they do—in a different department on the other side of the state from where they were confiscated.

Vehicles are sometimes donated, but they rarely come without strings attached. At the very least, the donor may be someone who has a speeding ticket he wants fixed. I know of one case in which a major car dealer presented a fleet of six new Cutlasses to a state agency for an even better reason: he wanted to know what they would be driving, since he also financed large drug deals behind the scenes. Even if you happen to run across one of the few people who are willing to shell out the cash for a vehicle out of the goodness of his heart, you risk him bragging about it. You don't really think he'll be able to resist telling his friends about his humanitarianism, do you? And then his friends will tell their friends, who'll tell their friends ...

Another way of dealing with the problem of getting vehicles, but which is usually limited to one-shot deals, is to borrow a vehicle from someone who is not connected with law enforcement. Most people love excitement—from a safe distance. It never ceases to amaze me how many otherwise sane human beings will readily turn over their keys in order to sit home and think about their car out fighting crime. Check for insurance problems before doing this, as there's always the chance that when you return Aunt Maudie's Honda Civic, the windshield will have been shot out.

If you work for a department that has a large budget, you face another set of problems. I'd practically stake my life on the fact that whoever is in charge of purchasing never did a day of undercover work in his life. But he's shrewd when it comes to a dollar, and he's looking for the most ride he can get for the bucks he has to put out. If he finds a dealer who'll cut the total price of six identical, hail-damaged, end-of-the-year sale Nissan Maximas by $2,000, yell, scream, threaten, beg, go over his head, around his side, or beneath his feet if necessary to stop him from buying them. As soon as one of those Maximas gets burned, they're all useless, and you might as well install bubble-gum lights on their roofs.

THE LIFE SPAN OF UNDERCOVER VEHICLES

To be honest, vehicles are a problem. They are expensive and have a very short "life" before they become suspect in a specific locality. Paint jobs and other cosmetic alterations help, but if word on the streets is that the narcs are driving a 1979 Corvette, it isn't going to make much difference if it changes from black to canary yellow. One solution to this dilemma is the development of a trading program with other departments in which cars, vans, trucks, and even airplanes make a circuit that never keeps them in one area very long.

There is always a chance that your vehicle will be suspected of belonging to a cop. This is one of the areas of undercover work where you don't just need a story and a reason to be there, you need a *damn good* story and reason. You and I know that there is more than one 1979 canary yellow 'Vette in the world, but we're not the problem. It's the bad guy who's jamming that 1911 Government Model down your throat who needs convincing.

Naturally, if you have any reason at all to suspect that your vehicle has been burned, don't drive it. Driving a car that doesn't fit your character is far better than driving one that may get shot at as you cruise down the street. Here, again, a good story is essential. If you're wearing one of those three-button pullover shirts with a little horse and rider on the left breast, and you are about to buy a load of Ecstasy from a guy named Skippy or Garth, you can still show up at the country club in a Taurus station wagon, if necessary. ("The fuel pump went out on my Beamer, dammit, and look what they stuck me with as a loaner!")

PREPARING UNDERCOVER VEHICLES

Regardless of what vehicle you choose to drive or how it is obtained, there are certain steps that must be taken to make it difficult, if not impossible, for the bad guys to find out who you really are.

License Tags

The first and most obvious thing to change is the license tag. All it takes to run your tag is one crack dealer whose brother-in-law is a patrolman. One dirty cop or civilian employee with access to the computer can do it just as well, and how many of us who aren't dirty haven't run a tag for a friend at one time or another? ("Hey, Jerry, you wouldn't believe the blond in the Camaro who smiled at me last night. If there's any way you could find out . . .")

Most large organizations make provisions for special tags to be used on their unmarked units. These tags are flagged in the computer, and any agency requesting registration information is told that the information is not on file. Then the agency that owns the vehicle is immediately notified that it is under scrutiny. This method works most of the time, since any cop who has ever worked traffic knows that for every car that is on file there seem to be about 16 that aren't. But a criminal who is smart enough to get a tag run is also smart enough to know how this system works, and if the registration check on your license tag comes back "not on file," the door to your identity opens even wider for speculation.

A method I always preferred was similar to one car thieves use. Find an amiable auto salvage dealer and pick up a few tags from him. Some can be local, but some should be from other states. If possible, take the tags from a vehicle that is the same make and model as the vehicle you will be driving. Run the tag yourself to ascertain who it is registered to, and your story will be that you just bought the car from that person. In these cases, the incredibly long lag time between the sale, title transfer, and entry of the new name into the state's computer files is a blessing rather than a curse.

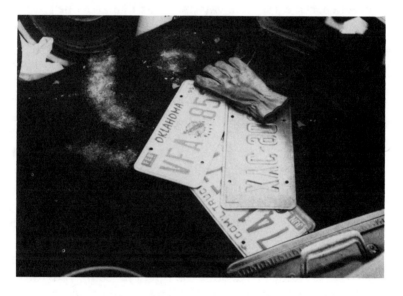

Carrying a variety of license plates in the trunk of your undercover vehicle may be more effective than displaying an agency tag that registers "not on file" in the computer. (Photo by Edward Hasbrook)

Finding license plates that come from the same model of vehicle that you will be driving is helpful but not essential. I drove a Ford Grenada for almost three years with Kansas plates that were registered to a Malibu SS. I was stopped once for speeding when I was alone, and my badge and a quick radio relay to my department explained the discrepancy. Had I been undercover at the time and in the company of a bad guy, so much the better. I'd have been busted for possession of a stolen vehicle, which would have added to the illusion I was creating. It could have been straightened out later, with spending a few hours in the county jail the only penalty. (This is no time to forget that you have a right to a phone call once you hit the jail, by the way.)

But beware. Your department may have a written policy against using tags from other vehicles. Find out if it does in advance, but do so in a way that doesn't alert your Homesteader supervisor to what you're up to. (Wait until he takes his shirts to the cleaners to be stuffed, then sneak a look at his policy manual. Why his? Because it'll be easy to find in the center of his desk, while yours was undoubtedly lost years ago.) The reason you need to find out about this policy clandestinely is that even if using tags from other vehicles is against the rules, you may decide to do it anyway.

Which introduces a theme that will recur throughout the rest of this book. Am I telling you to violate your department's policies? No, I'm telling you that you are constantly going to go head to head with the Homesteaders. They make the rules but have never worked undercover and don't know how the game is played. You're going to have to constantly balance your personal safety and the success of your cases against the threat of losing your job—and your pension.

Removing Cop-Like Items

Obviously, you don't want anything in or on your undercover vehicle that makes it look like it belongs to a cop. If the vehicle stays in your possession, it is easier to make sure of this than if other officers use it as well. Regardless, a detailed search of the entire vehicle should be conducted immediately before taking it undercover. Check for flashlights left under the seat and crumpled arrest warrants shoved in the glove compartment, and make sure that the handcuff key you dropped the other day isn't still on the floor.

Police Radios

As with many other aspects of undercover work, the experts are divided on whether an undercover vehicle should be equipped with a police radio. Some experts point out that the undercover officer needs to be able to communicate with his surveillance or backup team in the event that something goes wrong, and that the radio can be hidden in the trunk, inside a hollow console, or other places.

This is a nice thought, and if it makes you feel better to think that when the "feces hits the fan" you'll have time to get out of your car, open the trunk, call for help, and the backup team will arrive in time to save you, then maybe there's a good psychological reason for having a radio. But as far as I'm concerned, it's far more likely to hurt you than help you. I'd say the odds are about 1,000 to 1 that the bad guys will find your radio instead of it ever doing you any good.

Keep your head in the real world. No matter how close the members of your surveillance or backup team are, they aren't close enough. They will want to help, they will try to help, and many of them would even die to help you, but they won't be able to help you, because they won't get there in time. Never rely on your backup team. Learn to rely on yourself instead. When you're undercover, you're on your own.

TAKING CONTROL

I've talked about choosing a vehicle and getting it ready, but there's another aspect concerning your undercover vehicle that is the most important of all: you should always take *your* car any time you go somewhere with the bad guys. (There are exceptions, such as when you want a drug buy to go down in the suspect's vehicle in order to seize the vehicle.) There are many variables in an undercover assignment, and you should control everything you can from the beginning, including your transportation. The reason is obvious: if you pile into the backseat with a carload of crack-crazed addicts, you have no control over where you're going or what happens. They can take you anyplace they want to and do anything to you they please. And it would be a damn shame to see your wife in that line at the insurance office.

DRIVING

How you drive reveals as much about your character as what you drive. If you are one of those lucky souls who is 25 years old but still looks 18, and you find yourself planted in a high school somewhere, wondering how you're going to work undercover and pass Algebra II at the same time, by all means squeal those tires on that cherry red Camaro that the department gave you. But if you're graying at the temples and chauffeuring the boss to a triple martini lunch after a hard morning of corporate swindles, stay under the speed limit, come to a full stop at stop signs, and slow down to about two miles an hour at green lights on the off chance that they might turn yellow. (If you need lessons in this, I'll put you in touch with my father.)

CHAPTER 4

Undercover Overnight

Before you decide where you're going to lay your head down for the night, it would be wise to talk a little more about the different levels of undercover work. As previously discussed, at one extreme there are situations where it is advantageous for the officer to use his real name and the fact that he is a police officer, changing only the fact that he is honest. (I'm assuming here that you *are* honest, so don't disappoint me.) To even call this "light" undercover work is stretching it.

Next, there is what is commonly referred to as "decoy" work. Here the officer plays the part of a citizen rather than a criminal and creates the illusion that he is a likely victim for a crime. A good example of decoy work is San Diego's Border Crime Task Force of the late 1970s. During the 18 months this unit operated, officers masqueraded as illegal aliens to patrol the border south of San Diego where bandits robbed, raped, and murdered Mexicans crossing into the United States. Another prototype for successful decoy ops was the New York Police Department's (NYPD's) Stakeout Squad decoy unit led by Jim Cirillo. Cirillo and his men, also posing as civilians, stopped countless robberies in progress, prevented other crimes, and shot or arrested scores of violent criminals. Acting as a decoy is "heavy," very dangerous work. But the use of true undercover techniques in decoy operations is light, since they rarely involve extended contact with the bad guys.

At the other extreme is the heaviest undercover work, which is commonly referred to as "deep cover." When under deep cover, you move somewhere, set up shop under whatever guise you are using, and play the part of the bad guy 24 hours a day, seven days a week, 52 weeks a year. You may even get a job in order to brush shoulders with criminals. But no matter what you do, deep cover is time consuming and expensive unless you are working with a strong informant, in which case it is questionable whether deep cover is even necessary. There are times when it is, but those times are rare. To put it in business terms, the returns rarely justify the investment in time, money, and manpower.

Most undercover assignments fall somewhere between the two extremes. During most of the hours you work, you will not be undercover. Instead, you will be helping to organize operations, dealing with informants, and justifying your existence to the Homesteaders with ream after ream of paperwork. (You see, the Homesteaders have already caught on to the fact that you're having fun. Therefore, what you're doing can't possibly be work.) You will work primarily at night and return home after your shift to your little house with the white picket fence in the suburbs at about the time your children are leaving for school. You will drink coffee with your wife, and nod sleepily as she reminds you that you still have not fixed the leak in the bathroom or spoken to the neighbor who hasn't mowed his lawn in two weeks. In other words, most of the time you will still be living at home.

There will be occasions, however, when an operation keeps you away for more extended periods. How often this occurs depends to a large degree on whether you work for a local police or sheriff's department, a state agency, or the federal government. Generally, the smaller your jurisdictional area, the less frequently you will be gone overnight. But even if you're a detective for the Down Home, Arkansas, Police Department, you may hook up with a drug or burglary ring that has connections to San Francisco and New York. If you turn out to be the strongest inside man the hastily formed San Francisco/New York/Down Home task force has, you are likely to be boarding a plane for one of the coasts. And who knows? The Homesteader they call the Down Home Chief of Police might just let you go, especially if the SFPD or the NYPD foots the bill.

SHORT-TERM OVERNIGHT ASSIGNMENTS

For short-term overnight assignments, you will stay in hotels or motels, and your undercover billfold will be essential. Few hotels will book you a room without a credit card, or at least some kind of identification. If you're in New York or San Francisco and the bad guys don't know where you're staying, you can probably get by using your real name. But try this in Down Home and you'll find out that word in a small community gets around faster than Madonna and Bill Clinton combined. This can even happen in big cities with the right connections and the wrong luck. Can you imagine the blood rushing into your cheeks (if there's any of it left from that sucking bullet wound in your chest) as you stammer in embarrassment and try to explain to some guy known as Stiletto Sam why you registered under the name of a Down Home, Arkansas, cop?

If you are traveling with an informant, get two rooms if you intend to sleep. The downside to this is that you don't know what the informant is doing when he's in the other room. (I'll talk more about handling informants in Chapter 11, but for now I'll just say that you should never trust one completely and leave it at that.) The upside is that you can lock your door, stick your gun under the pillow, and be reasonably certain that you won't wake up with your jugular vein and carotid artery slashed to pieces. If you are traveling with a partner or linking up with another "good guy" after you arrive, sleeping in shifts will bypass this potential problem.

If it's bedtime and the bad guys are planning to sleep in the same room with you, or they will sleep in another room but have access to where you are sleeping, you have done something dreadfully stupid. That said, I will admit that I, myself, have done some dreadfully stupid things undercover at times, and this was one of them. I could tell you that it

Remember that there is more than one key to your motel room. Slipping a good jam under the door is an extra precaution that you can take. This one features a battery-operated alarm that sounds if the door is tried. (Photo by Jim Cash)

would be wise to stay awake all night, but if you have an IQ two points above that of a fence post, you know that without being told. If you don't and would even consider leaving yourself totally helpless among drug dealers, thieves, and murderers who may or may not know who you really are, forget undercover work right now. (I hear there's an opening for a Drug and Alcohol Resistance Education [DARE] officer. You should apply for it immediately.)

LONG-TERM OVERNIGHT ASSIGNMENTS

Only once in my career have I been set up in a house in another town and told to start hanging out in bars and making cases. (I'll discuss the ignorance and futility of such an arrangement later when I talk about dealing with infor-

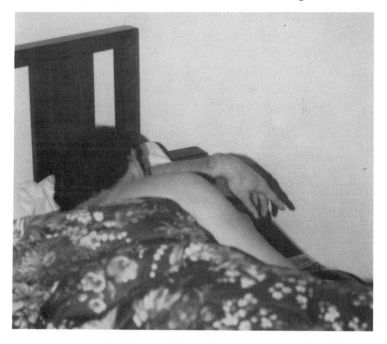

Neither a gun under your pillow nor a 99th-degree black belt will do you much good if the bad guys get to you while you're asleep. Unless you hear them in time to react, you won't ever wake up. (Photo by Jim Cash)

mants.) But if you get the wrong Homesteader running the show, you may find yourself in such a predicament, so let's talk about choosing houses or apartments.

Where to Live

To begin with, the house you choose, like everything else, should blend well with the overall illusion you are creating. For instance, if you're supposed to be a down-on-his-luck junkie, you can't afford to rent the penthouse at the Manhattan Plaza now, can you? But if you're a posing as a pharmaceutical salesman, and you're trying to catch a doctor who's writing Valium prescriptions faster than a Jehovah's Witness delivers the *Watchtower*, you aren't going to take up residence in a roach-infested pay-by-the-week flophouse. Wherever you choose to live, consider it the home of your undercover personality, not you.

Your choice of housing must blend with your undercover character. Ask yourself who would live there: a down-on-his-luck junkie or a high-dollar dealer? (Photo by Jim Cash)

Keeping the Place Clean

I don't care how often you vacuum, dust, or scrub your toilet. What I mean by keeping your place clean is making sure that nothing that even remotely connects you with police work comes through your front door. (Leave the handcuffs and collapsible batons at your real home.) This includes the straight cops who are your contacts with the real world. Call them on a pay phone, meet them somewhere safe, or tell them to go to hell if you want to, but don't let them come around your undercover house. If the bad guys know where you live and have any suspicions at all, they will be watching you.

Friends or Business Associates?

Again, I must stress that this is a dumb and dangerous way to go about trying to make cases. Because if you find yourself living in a house under an undercover name, hanging out in bars, and trying to meet bad guys, you are going to have to represent yourself as their friend rather than someone who just wants to do business. Creating the illusion that you are a business associate of criminals is a piece of cake compared to presenting yourself as their friend. Criminal business associates do criminal business together and then go home to their different lives. Criminal friends hang out, get drunk, use drugs, and have sex with whores together. (Do I have to point out the obvious problems that can arise from this?) Worst of all, friends come over to visit, and if they are criminal friends, they bring their booze, dope, and whores with them. If you think that brother-in-law of yours who camped out on your sofa for six weeks after his divorce was hard to get rid of, wait until you get a bunch of speed freaks crashing on your living-room floor.

The displeasure you will experience, however, is the least of your worries. Sooner or later, one of the meth heads is going to come across the stub from your last paycheck because you got lazy and didn't follow directions about keeping such things out of the house. Or he's going to catch on to the fact that you aren't using any dope yourself. Or the burglars who brought over the bucket of Kentucky Fried Chicken are going to need a driver to take them to their next job, and you're not going to have any way to alert the straight cops that you're about to become a "wheel man."

To summarize, whether it's for one night or two years, you must take extra precautions to ensure your safety when you are undercover and sleeping away from home. Even if you have a 99th-degree black belt in every martial art known to man, two dozen S&W Model 29 .44 Magnums under your pillow, and an M60 mounted on the motel room desk facing the door, you are as vulnerable as a newborn baby when you are asleep. Take this seriously. Really. It could save your life.

PART

2

GETTING INTO CHARACTER

CHAPTER 5

Rehearsing Your New Identity

Writers create characters. Actors portray them. As an undercover officer, you do both. By now you should have completed the "writer's" part of creating an undercover identity and personality. You know what your fictitious name will be, and you have at least a general grasp of the character's temperament and demeanor. It is now time to move from writer to actor and learn to become the person you have created.

SUBJECTIVITY AND OBJECTIVITY

Working effectively undercover involves both subjectivity and objectivity. Subjectively, you must feel the emotions that your character experiences. Human beings have some reaction to everything that they encounter in their environment. Small reactions go unseen by others, while large reactions can be quite dramatic. The responses people witness in you when you are undercover must be appropriate to your character rather than yourself.

Study how you respond to what goes on around you. Ask yourself a few questions. What do you do when you're in a hurry but get caught in a traffic jam? Do you scream at the top of your lungs and bang on the steering wheel in frustration, or sit quietly, stewing as you wait? Does your undercover character do the same thing, or does he react differently? Picture yourself walking along a sidewalk without a jacket. The sun suddenly goes behind a cloud, and the temperature drops 10 degrees. Do you shiver, make a big deal out of it, and decide that returning home for your coat must take priority over everything else, or do you shrug your shoulders and accept the fact that you'll probably be a little colder today than you'd planned? How would the character you have created react?

At the same time that you are subjectively learning to feel the emotions of your undercover character, you must remain objective. Never forget that in reality, you are a cop who is watching, noting, and remembering the details of what is going on around you so you can later write an intelligent report and testify in court. This may seem a little silly to you, because what I am really saying is don't forget who you really are. That seems pretty impossible, doesn't it? Well, just wait until you have successfully mastered the art of getting into character and actually taking on the undercover personality you have created, and you will see what I mean.

I recall a college friend of mine, Larry, who was a drama major and also a member of the basketball team. Larry was in a play in which he portrayed an Englishman and spoke with a British accent. It was fun to watch him play basketball, because he was an excellent point guard. But it was even more fun to go to the games as the play neared opening night, because Larry would run down the court shouting to his teammates in a British accent.

Larry had allowed his subjectivity to infiltrate his objectivity. I don't mean he really thought he was an Englishman, but the line he had established between reality and fantasy grew a little less clear than it should have.

THE BALANCING ACT

Your subjectivity and objectivity must remain balanced throughout your undercover assignment, as too much emphasis on either can be destructive to your case and possibly to you. If you get too far into your character (subjectivity), you will have problems later when you try to recall the details of the case. But too much objectivity can cause a superficial performance, which will destroy your credibility and create doubt in the eyes of the bad guys.

Sound difficult? I won't lie to you—it ain't easy. At least not at first. As with anything else you desire to master, you must practice, practice, and then practice some more. Experience is the only way to ensure that this seemingly "split" personality becomes second nature. But you may not be able to acquire enough experience as your character, which is something stage and screen actors don't have to worry about.

The hard, cold fact is that a poor opening-night performance for the bad guys can lead to more grievous consequences than if an audience walks out during Act I. You've got to be convincing in your undercover role from the moment your beard goes on, or you stand a chance of blowing a case and getting hurt. Therefore, it makes sense to get as comfortable as possible with your new character before you go undercover for the first time.

PRACTICE

Some of the following exercises may seem unnecessary and even stupid at first. I assure you they are valuable learning tools. They are designed so you can perform them privately or with a trusted partner, so you won't have to endure the raised eyebrows of the Homesteaders or watch them make notes about you in those little spiral notebooks they like to keep.

Exercise #1:

In the morning when you wake up, before you open your eyes, envision yourself as your undercover character. What are you wearing? How do you feel? What did you do last night?

Then, with your eyes still closed, envision yourself waking up in another bedroom. (Yes, it can be Cindy Crawford's bedroom if you like, but don't let her get in the way of the rest of the exercise.) Take note of the details in that room: What kind of bed are you in? What do the curtains look like? Is the floor carpeted or wooden? Is there a dresser? A chest of drawers? What else?

Open your eyes. Being objective and subjective simultaneously, try to see both your bedroom and the room you just created.

Staying in character, get out of bed. Does your undercover character get out of bed the same way you do? How does the character walk when he first gets up and heads to the bathroom for his toothbrush? Brush your teeth in character. Does your character brush up and down, sideways, or both?

Perform the rest of your character's morning rituals, not yours. For instance, you may not eat breakfast, but does your undercover character?

Continue this exercise throughout the day, as long as it is practical. When you finish, break out of character, sit down at your desk, and write as detailed a report as you can about the exercise.

Exercise #2:

While seated at your desk, which should have a phone book on it, close your eyes and take a few seconds to become your undercover character.

Then open your eyes, and reach for the phone book the way your character would. Open it the way he would open it, turn to the Yellow Pages section, and find the listing for Apartments for Rent.

Pick up the phone the way your character would, and dial the first listing. Identify yourself by your undercover name, and begin asking the questions that a person who is interested in renting an apartment would ask: Are the apartments furnished or unfurnished? What is the monthly rent for a one-bedroom unit? A two-bedroom unit? A three-bedroom unit? How about a fireplace—does the complex have them? On what day of the month is the rent due? Can special arrangements be made to pay the rent on a day that coincides more favorably with your character's pay schedule? Who pays the gas and electric bills, the tenant or the management? Who pays for water and trash collection? How long is the lease, and what does it entail?

As you ask questions, be prepared to answer questions that are asked of you: Where do you work? Where do you live now? Do not break character under any circumstances. If you are asked something to which you have no precon-

This future undercover operative is taking the first step toward feeling comfortable with her new character: calling apartment houses under a new and awkward-feeling identity. (Photo by Edward Hasbrook)

ceived answer, don't panic and hang up. Cover it any way you can. You're going to be doing a lot of that in the future, so get used to it now.

As soon as you hang up, evaluate your performance. If everything went smoothly, that's nice, but you probably didn't learn anything. Repeat this exercise by calling other apartment complexes. Don't worry about wasting the manager's time. (I managed a large apartment complex for awhile. There isn't that much to it, and they probably even appreciate the break in monotony.)

Exercise #3:

As soon as you feel comfortable with the phone calls you've made, make an appointment to look at one or more of the apartments that you inquired about. When you meet the manager or whoever will be showing you the apartment, introduce yourself using your undercover name. (The more you use this name, the more natural it will begin to feel.) As you are led through the rooms, look at them the way your undercover character would. Is it important to your character that the carpet is frayed? Do the nail holes in the wall that were left by the last tenant bother him? Is the kitchen adequate? How about storage space?

Ask to see more than one unit, if possible, repeating pertinent questions each time for more practice. At first, you will feel uneasy and suspect that the person showing you the apartments knows you are not who you profess to be. But as you continue, you will begin to realize that most people accept things at face value and do not question what they are told unless they have some reason to. Your job is to never give them a reason.

Finally, return to the manager's office and get an application to rent an apartment. Unless you have really decided to rent the apartment for some reason, look at your watch, say you are running late, and tell the manager that you will take the application with you to fill out and return later.

Back at your office or at home, fill out the application

Posing as a potential renter provides face-to-face contact using your undercover personality. (Photo by Edward Hasbrook)

with facts pertinent to your undercover identity. Seeing them on paper will help solidify the character in your mind. And who knows? You may find a better place to live than that dump you're in now.

Exercise #4:

Make a list of questions that includes name, age, occupation, address, telephone number, level of education, and so on. At the end of each question, leave space to write in an answer. When you are finished, memorize the list, then stick it in a drawer of your desk.

Pick a bar, club, lounge, or restaurant where you are not known and, assuming your undercover identity, go inside. Arbitrarily pick out a person (not the bartender—that's too easy) and strike up a conversation. Using the questions from the list, learn as much about your subject as you can. Do not be so direct that you arouse suspicion; you must talk in generalities and gradually lead your subject to talk about the areas of his life in which you are interested. You'll be walking a very fine line indeed, and your subject's distrust may be aroused quickly. In your objective role as a cop, you should constantly monitor your subject to see if you are stepping over that line.

At the same time that you are trying to learn as much as you can about the person you have chosen, try not to reveal anything more about yourself than what is necessary to keep

This officer is trying valiantly to remember the questions he wrote on the paper in his desk drawer. At the same time he attempts to learn as much as possible about his practice subject, he tries to give away little about himself. (Photo by Edward Hasbrook)

the conversation going. After creating an undercover character, the officer may be inclined to speak more freely than the average person would in a situation like this. (You mean you wrote that whole biography, and now you don't even get to use it? Yes. The purpose of writing down the details of your character's life was more to make you feel comfortable in your role than for the benefit of the bad guys.)

When you have gained as much information from your subject as you can, return to your office, pull the list of questions out of your desk, and begin filling in the blanks. How many of the questions are you able to answer? How many did you forget to ask? How many of the questions do you remember the subject answering but you can't remember what the answer was?

Critique your performance. At any point did you get the impression that the person was wondering why you were so curious? If so, what had you done to arouse his suspicion?

If you repeat this exercise several times, you will soon find that people speak about themselves with varying degrees of freedom. Some are quiet and reserved, and others are gregarious braggarts, but the majority fall somewhere in between. What you must do is find a "key" that will enable you to establish common ground with each person you encounter. By doing this, you will gain that person's confidence.

On occasion, you will get the impression that you are being lied to, and if you do, you probably are. Average people do a fair amount of lying about their lives—especially to people they've just met. Sometimes it is because they don't trust strangers, but more often it is because they perceive the truth as boring, or they're ashamed of what they consider to be their failures.

For your purposes, the reasons average people lie make little difference. What you must remember is that criminals lie even more than average people, and regardless of how insignificant it might seem, every bit of information you obtain while undercover should be checked out and substantiated by another source.

Exercise #5:
Pick one of the people you met while performing exercise #4. Using the information from the questionnaire you filled out, try to locate him or her again. (If any of them were attractive members of the opposite sex, you've probably already

thought of this, you dog, you.) Sounds easy enough, right? After all, you're a trained, experienced investigator. Well, there's a little fly I'm going to throw into the ointment here. You've got to locate your subject without him or her finding out that you are doing so.

Confirm through a second source all addresses, phone numbers, places of employment, and other bits of intelligence you obtained. Some of your confirmations can be made over the phone, but you should make a point to conduct at least some face-to-face interviews. Keep in mind that your subject is likely to remember your face if you perform this exercise too soon after doing exercise #4. To avoid the obvious problem of the subject identifying you while you are checking out his or her stories, the name you use, both over the phone and in person, should not be your real name or that of your undercover character.

At this point, you might begin thinking about developing a secondary undercover identity to be used in situations

People lie, so corroboration of intelligence is a must. This is where a secondary undercover character is often helpful. (Photo by Edward Hasbrook)

like this. This identity need not be as ingrained as your primary character, but you should know the character well enough to step into his shoes for short periods of time. John Wesley Lanier served this purpose for me, and at various times "Wes" played the role of meter reader, newspaper reporter, insurance investigator, and bum. (Yes, I know I'm supposed to call them homeless now, but Wes was a bum.)

Exercise #6:

Open a newspaper to the classifieds section and find the help wanted listings. Skim the list of job openings until you find one that you believe both you and your undercover character could perform, then call the number and make an appointment for an interview. Do your homework before each interview. If the job requires a master's degree in biology and you don't have one, invent one from a university that has a biology department.

The job interview is perhaps the most difficult of the training exercises. This officer is attempting to convince her potential employer that a totally fictitious character not only exists, but should be hired. (Photo by Edward Hasbrook)

At the interview, do your very best to impress the interviewer with your qualifications, using your undercover identity, of course. Before the interview, you will need to come up with some reason you can't take the job in case you are hired on the spot. (Unless it happens to pay more than police work—and what doesn't?)

Repeat this exercise with other job openings. Gradually move from applying for jobs you know something about to areas in which you have little or no knowledge. This will increase the difficulty of the exercise and require you to rely more on your verbal abilities (read that BS abilities) than actual experience, which is exactly what undercover work is all about.

The exercises above were designed to have increasing degrees of difficulty and inherent tension. If you fail to brush your teeth as your undercover character would in exercise #1, only you will know. But if the apartment manager you speak to on the phone in exercise #2 suspects that you are being less than honest, you will feel embarrassed when you hang up the phone.

Exercises #3 and #4 involve face-to-face contact, which increases the potential for embarrassment and adds the possibility that your practice subject will get suspicious enough to write down the license tag of your vehicle. (If this happens, you may find yourself sitting in your supervisor's office trying to explain why you are playing games with honest citizens and using their tax dollars to do so. As a Homesteader, he is probably not going to understand that it is part of your undercover training.)

The last two exercises increase the stakes to even higher levels. In exercise #5, you must investigate someone who is most likely guilty of no crime, and honest Americans who learn that the police are checking up on them without good reason can become irritated enough to cause you problems. In exercise #6, you must out-and-out misrepresent yourself and waste time for somebody who needs to hire someone to do a job. He may be angry enough to file a complaint if he learns the truth.

In other words, if you screw up and get caught performing these exercises, you are very likely to have some trouble. That's precisely why I use them to train undercover officers, and that's why I included them in this book. Knowing there may be negative consequences if you get burned should create a certain degree of anxiety—anxiety that is similar to the fear you will sometimes experience undercover.

You are going to experience fear undercover because you'll be aware that faulty performances in front of bad guys have more severe consequences than getting tripped up misrepresenting yourself to an apartment manager. That fear is going to be far more severe than the minor little jitters you get when doing these exercises. So you might as well start learning to recognize, deal with, and work through this "friendly" fear now. Don't look at fear as a negative thing. Fear is a natural instinct that prepares human beings for "fight or flight" responses. In an undercover situation, it can be the early warning that gives you a split-second edge, which can mean the difference between life and death.

Take time to get out of character when these exercises (and later, the undercover assignments) are over. Extreme intensity, long periods undercover, and fatigue can make this more difficult than you might think. Remember Larry, the British basketball player? I had my own similarly embarrassing experience one Thanksgiving after my partner and I had worked undercover for two days straight without sleep. About to nod off, I was still Mickey Jordan when my wife and I arrived at her parents' house for dinner. Mickey sat down, listened to a very nice prayer from his in-laws' minister, who had joined the family for the holiday, and promptly said, "Now, will somebody please pass the motherfuckin' turkey. I'm hungry."

CHAPTER 6

Advanced Training

Just how good an undercover officer do you want to be? Do you want to be able to perform adequately, collect your salary, and go home? Or would you like to be great?

Regardless of what profession they choose, most people settle for mediocrity in their work. Those who don't and go on to set new standards have several characteristics in common. They are intelligent, self-motivated, creative, and no matter how many times it appears that they have failed, they never accept defeat. They possess at least a little natural talent for what they do, but, far more important than that, they have figured out the mysterious, elusive secret of success: WORK. Before you suspect that I've given up undercover work and am now conducting motivational seminars for Amway, I must tell you that I truly believe that if you study the techniques in this book and combine them with practical undercover experience, you will become a good undercover officer.

But there's another secret that successful people know,

which has to do with education. It is the fact that nobody can really teach you anything. Instructors, whether they present their material in person, on video, or on the pages of a book, can do little more than touch on their complex subjects, hope you absorb the high points, and point you in the right direction so you can continue to teach yourself.

In other words, undercover work has far too many facets, intricate little details, sidelines, rules, and exceptions to the rules to explore in a hundred volumes. If you really want to master undercover work, you will have to accept the fact that self study is your only option. And, like any good teacher will do, I will do my best to open the door to self education for you and even shove you through if I have to.

EDUCATION

You should take advantage of all courses offered by the DEA, BATF, state police, or anyone else. Some courses are extremely good, others are mediocre, and I have taken a few that sucked big time. But I have never been to from which I didn't learn something, even if it was by negative example. As you learn and gain practical experience in working undercover, you will be able to separate the wheat from the chaff. You will quickly spot the teachers who are nothing more than teachers and have no undercover experience themselves. (Warning: Homesteaders sometimes plant their crops in the teaching field.) In short, you will learn to keep what is beneficial and discard what is not only idiotic but potentially dangerous.

In the days when I was a young undercover cop, the term "educated idiot" was used to describe any officer who was even thinking about college. The consensus was that all it took to be a good law enforcement officer was common sense. You either had it or you didn't, and no amount of training was going to change that reality. However, as departments, bureaus, and agencies stiffened the educational requirements for applicants, and some of the more narrow-minded old-timers retired and entered exciting new careers as night watchmen and janitors, it became obvious that education and common sense were not mutually exclusive.

While "book learnin'," as they used to call it, will never be as valuable as hands-on experience in any field, there is absolutely no reason not to get as much of both as you possibly can. Experience must be acquired on the job, but there are many avenues to getting an education. I'll explore a few that relate directly to the education of undercover officers.

Drama Classes

Any university that has a drama department can be an invaluable educational tool. Look for classes with titles like Beginning Acting or Principles of Stagecraft. At first, you may feel a little odd sitting on the floor in front of the other students and pretending to be a snowflake, or a can of green beans, or an orangutan. But if you stick it out you'll

Drama classes and stage experience, with a heavy emphasis on the improvisational styles of acting, are equally valuable training for the undercover officer as anything offered at the police academy. (Photo by Edward Hasbrook)

find that your undercover performances become more convincing—and more bad guys go to jail.

A class in theater makeup can teach you how you can change your appearance convincingly, and, more importantly, how you can't. Speech classes, particularly those that emphasize impromptu speaking, can instill confidence in you as well as expose you to the stress of speaking in front of an audience. Use good judgment when enrolling—you may want to enroll using your undercover identity in order to maintain anonymity.

I switched my undergraduate major to criminal justice after spending two years as a drama major. Drama eventually became my minor, and at the time I received my bachelor of arts (BA) degree, I was the only person who'd ever graduated from the small state college I attended with this unusual major and minor combination. Unusual? Certainly. But a perfect combination for an undercover officer. I couldn't have picked a better one even if I'd had the sense to know what I was doing.

Speech classes can make the officer more comfortable in front of a crowd. While the skills are not as directly transferable to the stress of undercover work, the dynamics are similar. (Photo by Edward Hasbrook)

Experience

For undercover officers, acting classes and experience are at least as valuable as law enforcement training, and probably more so. If you can arrange your shift schedule to attend rehearsals, you should audition for a part in the next production put on by your local community theater. Again, it may be wise to try out using your undercover name rather than publicize the fact that you are a police officer.

A word should be interjected at this point concerning the moral obligation that goes with your steadily increasing proficiency in role camouflage. By now you are beginning to see that the ability to change your identity as easily as you do your underwear carries with it certain advantages, and if you are at all human, sooner or later you will be tempted to abuse this power. Remember that undercover work entails both subjectivity and objectivity. If you accept a part in a play, the other members of the cast will count on you to show up for rehearsals and hold up your end of the bargain, regardless of what name they know you by. Such moral obligations apply to any responsibility you take on under another name and even extends to more serious matters, which will be discussed in Part 5 on traps.

Improvisation

While all acting classes and experience are good training, those that emphasize improvisational styles are more beneficial to the undercover officer than others. The popularity of *Saturday Night Live*, *Second City Television*, and similar TV shows in the last two decades has brought about an increase in the number of classes that are offered on this sub-craft.

Improvisational acting is exactly what undercover work is all about. You do not have a script from which to work but rather a basic plot scenario. The dialogue must be created as you go, and the actors, rather than a playwright, determine the course that the story will take. This means that you must remain alert and ready to respond to the other people "on stage." In order to maintain control of the situation, you must guide the plot in the direction you want it to go (leading to an illicit drug sale or the revealing of information, for example), and you must do this as convincingly as Richard Burton or Dame Edith Evans if you don't want the show to close with a bang on opening night.

Commedia Dell'arte

One of the most beneficial drama classes I ever took was a course called Styles of Acting. We spent a good part of the semester studying and performing commedia dell'arte, an Italian renaissance drama form in which only a skeletal outline of the play is provided. The actors create the dialogue, fill in the details, and invent subplots as the story unfolds. In other words, the performers have a general task to accomplish, but the script does not spell out exactly how it is to be accomplished. This is precisely what you do as an undercover "actor," with the exception that most commedia dell'arte was whimsical farce. (But don't think for a minute that undercover work doesn't have its farcical moments.)

Commedia dell'arte was performed by traveling companies of actors who often specialized in stock roles. These plays often took unexpected turns. (Does this sound familiar? Inventing appropriate dialogue on the spur of the moment, reacting spontaneously to other actors, improvising sections of a scene, and following unexpected turns, but still pulling the story back toward the specific end you want it to have—this is what undercover work is all about.) A typical plot scenario reads something like the following:

Pantalone (the elderly and suspicious husband of the beautiful, young Columbina) arrives home to find a man's hat sitting on the table. From the bedroom, he hears the sounds of passionate lovemaking. He walks toward the sounds but is cut off by Arlechino, who has entered from a side room to block the bedroom door. (Arlechino is Pantalone's unscrupulous servant, whom he suspects is carrying on an affair with Columbina.) Arlechino smiles and talks rapidly to his master, waving both hands wildly behind his back. It is obvious that he is attempting to stall Pantalone and signal to someone in the bedroom.

Pantalone demands to know who is making love to his wife. Arlechino says he does not know, but they will go into the bedroom together and kill the dastardly fellow. He then reminds Pantalone that he has accused him of such treachery in the past. Pantalone apologizes profusely to Arlechino and admits he must have been wrong—Columbina's lover is someone else. He begs his servant's forgiveness.

Arlechino then distracts the gullible Pantalone and leads him across the room. They busy themselves at the table discussing the hat. When the old man finally remembers his wife, he starts for the bedroom door again, but before he can enter, Columbina walks out. Her clothes are in disarray, and her hair is unkempt. Pantalone confronts her, but she protests that no one was in the bedroom with her. Pantalone keeps trying to enter the bedroom, but both Arlechino and Columbina block his path in a series of movements designed to look like clumsy accidents.

As this continues, a partially-clad man, the captain (another stock character), runs past a side window from the rear of the house. Pantalone is facing away from the window and does not see him. Arlechino hurries out of the house as Columbina continues to block Pantalone from the bedroom. The captain runs past the window back toward the rear of the house as Arlechino reenters, and Pantalone misses him again. The captain runs by the window several more times, but each time

Pantalone is distracted in some way, and Arlechino must retrieve the captain for another try.

Finally, both Arlechino and Columbina grab Pantalone and stick his head out the window as the captain runs by carrying his pants. Pantalone finally sees the captain, assumes him to be Columbina's lover, and hobbles off in angry pursuit. The scene closes with Arlechino and Columbina laughing hysterically, and then Arlechino lifts Columbina into his arms and carries her into the bedroom.

As you can see from the script, few of the details are spelled out and must be improvised on the spot. You can steal a few ideas from this classic Italian acting style and put them to your own use. Before you go out on a typical

The purpose of writing a scenario that describes how you want an undercover assignment to progress is similar to the one for writing a biography for your undercover personality—it instills the details in your mind. Remember that nothing ever goes exactly as planned, and be ready to change your strategy if necessary. (Photo by Edward Hasbrook)

drug buy, take the information you have and write a scenario for it in the style of commedia dell'arte. It might be
something like this:

> A little before lunchtime, Detective Jones will
> accompany confidential informant Mike Williams to
> the office of Joe Bloom, a real estate agent and sus-
> pected cocaine dealer. Williams will introduce
> Detective Jones as "Tom Smith," an old friend of his
> from the Minneapolis/St. Paul area. Williams will
> also inform Bloom that Jones (Smith) wants to pur-
> chase cocaine.
>
> Bloom and Jones will discuss price, and then
> Williams will say that he is hungry and suggest that
> they all go to lunch and do the deal afterwards.
> (Williams maintains that Bloom transports the
> drugs in his late-model Cadillac Seville, and Jones
> wants to obtain proof of this in order to seize the
> vehicle as well as arrest Bloom after the buy.)
>
> Jones and Williams will ask Bloom to suggest a
> place to go for lunch, using the excuse that Bloom
> knows the area better than they do. They are hopeful
> that Bloom will also offer to drive, and that the buy
> and subsequent arrest can go down in the Cadillac.
>
> Detective Jones' primary goal is the illegal pur-
> chase of cocaine from Bloom. His secondary goal is
> to manage the buy in a manner that will provide
> evidence that Bloom's Cadillac is used in the trans-
> portation of the controlled substance, which will
> lead to its seizure.

This is the plan. Suppose that everything goes according to Hoyle in the real estate office, but as they step out of
the building and start to head toward the Cadillac, our old
friend Murphy raises his ugly head and exclaims that it's
time for his law to come into effect. Bloom glances at his
watch and remembers he has an early afternoon appoint-

ment to show a house. He suggests they eat a quick lunch at the diner just down the block—within walking distance.

Jones must decide how important it is that the deal goes down in the car. Will he still have enough evidence to seize the vehicle if he sees Bloom go to the Cadillac and return with some type of container, from which he later produces cocaine? What if Bloom goes to the car, gets in, and returns with his hands empty and the cocaine concealed on his person? Can Jones still swear under oath that the cocaine came from the Cadillac? Jones must also decide how important it is that the vehicle is seized. Is it worthwhile to press the issue, take the chance of making Bloom suspicious, and risk blowing the whole buy?

These are judgment calls that can only be made by Jones. They must be made quickly, on the spot, with only his instincts to guide him. If he is an experienced undercover officer and sensitive to Bloom's reactions and attitudes, it is likely that his intuition will be good and he will make the right decisions.

Jones could decide that the only way to ensure that the deal goes down in the car is to insist that they eat at another place. But Bloom has already stated that he doesn't have time for this, so for Jones and Williams to make a big deal out of it would be inappropriate. So Jones agrees to eat at the diner. And God, who looks after drunks, fools, and undercover officers, smiles on him.

After lunch, Bloom, Jones, and Williams walk back to the real estate office parking lot. Bloom opens the trunk of the Cadillac and pulls out a briefcase, and the three men reenter the office. Bloom then opens the briefcase, pulls out an ounce of coke, and the buy goes down. Jones arrests Bloom, and since he witnessed the briefcase being taken from the Cadillac, and the briefcase eventually proved to contain cocaine, he is able to seize the vehicle as well.

This has been a drama with three scenes: 1) the initial discussion of the cocaine purchase at the office, 2) lunch at the diner, and 3) the actual buy/bust at the office. The scenario is typical of most undercover operations in that not everything went the way Jones had hoped, but by remaining flexible and keeping control of the situation, he still made the case.

But there are perhaps a thousand other ways this little drama could have gone down. For example, when they returned to the parking lot after lunch, Bloom could have sent Jones and Williams into his office and opened the Cadillac trunk privately. Would Jones have been able to swear under oath that the vehicle was involved in the transaction? Not unless he was lucky enough to witness the briefcase being taken from the car through a window from inside Bloom's office. What if Jones had insisted that they go somewhere else to eat? Could he have come up with a story that sounded legitimate? Jones could have said that he heard that someone got ptomaine poisoning from eating at the diner, or he owed money to someone who frequented the place and didn't want to take the chance of bumping into him. But both stories sound pretty thin and, to a certain degree, contradict the basis for which Jones and Williams wanted Bloom to pick the lunch site in the first place: Bloom knows the area better than they do.

Jones made a pretty good decision, if you ask me. He was willing to sacrifice the seizure of the vehicle in order to make the case, and in the end, he was lucky and got both. That was because he controlled the situation as best he could by guiding what transpired toward the end he wanted. He was also prepared for unexpected events, willing to cut his losses if necessary, and capable of thinking on his feet. I suspect that Detective Jones had a great deal of good, solid experience in undercover work. I also suspect that he had taken advantage of every educational opportunity he could find to perfect his craft.

Go thee and do likewise.

PART 3

WORKING THE VARIOUS CRIMES

CHAPTER 7

Narcotics and Other Illegal Drugs

While nearly any criminal investigation can benefit from the correct use of undercover officers, some crimes are more readily associated with clandestine operations than others. At the very top of the list is the illegal possession, purchase, and sale of controlled substances—this is the crime the public most closely associates with police undercover work.

IMAGE

The suggestion of illegal street drugs conjures up Hollywood images of bearded, earringed Al Pacino or Keanu Reeves look-alike drug dealers, who have testicles the size of basketballs and fear nothing. Hollywood has given most people a fairly warped perception of undercover narcotics officers, too. They imagine a handsome adventurer with a devil-may-care attitude, racing his convertible through the streets after the bad guys. He's probably accompanied by a physically flawless female officer (large and perfectly formed breasts are a must), who dresses like a slut but also has class, making it clear that the slut image is only for the job. She's in frequent danger of being raped, and, if it were 10 years ago, our male hero would have had to save her virtue at least once per episode. Nowadays, she saves herself, but the sexual danger overtones are still there. (You've come a long way, baby.) The high-tech, high-capacity 9mm automatic pistols carried by both man and woman ride in flashy horizontal shoulder holsters—which are useless, if not dangerous, in undercover work—and other unproductive equipment that no knowledgeable narc would be caught dead having hanging from his belt: handcuffs, pepper spray, and collapsible batons. This is topped off with some sort of exotic rifle or shotgun system in the backseat (one of those new Star-Wars-looking things that the average cop might mistake for a kitchen appliance rather than a weapon).

Well, folks, it ain't just Hollywood. These men and women do exist in the world of undercover work, but the difference is that while these types of individuals are admired on TV, they're usually the subject of great ridicule by other undercover specialists. Narcotics undercover work is fun and exciting, but don't ever let it go to your head. You aren't as tough, cool, or handsome as you think you are. (The only person who thinks I look like Tom Selleck is me.)

The basic rule of appearance in narcotics investigation is no different from that for any other undercover operation: look like what you're supposed to be, not what *Miami Vice* told you to look like. The average narcotics dealer doesn't look like a movie star, and neither should you. But how you look isn't nearly as important as how you act.

Dopers come in all sizes, shapes, forms, and from all walks of life. Members of different subcultures and ethnic groups do drug business with one another, so with the right story, you should be able to look like Malcolm X and buy speed from the Ku Klux Klan. Of course, there's no reason

Good undercover stories enable officers of different ages, ethnic backgrounds, and economic environments to branch out and do business at all levels. This middle-aged narcotics investigator was introduced to the teenager by an informant. He wants to see "what all the fuss is about marijuana." The kids may laugh at the old fart after he's gone, but they won't turn down his money. (Photo by Edward Hasbrook)

to do this if you don't have to. But all in all, your appearance is very much like talent: it's nice to have talent, but it doesn't take the place of work. And when you go undercover, it's nice to look the part but far more important that you play it well.

The image you portray when purchasing narcotics or other controlled substances should be directly related to what you buy and the size of the buy. In general, if you show up on the wrong side of the tracks and ask for one bag of marijuana, you will be labeled a user. If you meet a contact in order to discuss a 200-kilo purchase, however, you will be labeled a dealer, and you may or may not also be a user.

INFORMANTS

The key to all undercover work, and drug buys in particular, is your informant. Without strong informants, you will have little or no success at making cases. Going in cold is more than just a waste of time—it can be hazardous to your health. At the very least, it can get you burned and blow your case.

Ignore the small county sheriff who claims that "if you go hang out in that bar on the edge of town, they'll just throw the dope at you." Let's be reasonable here. A new face shows up in a small town and starts asking strangers where he can score? Give me a break. And give the dope dealers some credit, too. If they're that stupid, they aren't dealing very big lots and won't be in business long anyway.

The shadowed figure in the Chevy Blazer behind the table is a narcotics investigator who stumbled on this buy in progress. With no informant to introduce him, the investigator has chosen to use his undercover identity in a surveillance mode and obtain intelligence. (Photo by Edward Hasbrook)

Ask yourself how much damage a drug dealer at this level is doing, and whether or not your time might be better spent on smarter dealers elsewhere.

There are exceptions to every rule, of course, and if you go in cold often enough and don't get your throat cut, eventually you are going to find someone who'll sell you a small amount of some illegal drug. But it's not going to be a major buy, and it's definitely not going to be worth the time you invested. Undercover drug operations are like anything else in life: you have to get your priorities straight. An undercover officer has 24 hours in a day, 7 days in a week, and 52 weeks in a year just like everybody else. If you spend six weeks gaining the confidence of some penny-ante idiot drug dealer when you could make 100 better cases in that period of time by using an informant, all you prove is that you are a penny-ante idiot yourself.

The average drug deal has many twists and turns and variations—too many to cover every possible one here. But, in general, most drug deals follow the same basic formula. Remember the story of Adam and Eve in the Preface? God didn't have to use an informant to find out that Adam had eaten of the Forbidden Fruit. That's because He's God. He just knew. I hate to break the news to you, but you aren't, and you don't. This means your first step is to acquire an informant who has connections to the world of illegal drugs. How you obtain and maintain the informant's services varies, but, for the most part, informants come in four categories:

The Good Citizen. The good-citizen informant is just what his name implies: a good citizen who wants to help the police rid the streets of pushers, pimps, robbers, rapists, and other subhumans. His strength is his honesty, but it is also his weakness. If he really is a good citizen, he isn't likely to have the criminal connections he needs to help you. And if he does appear to have those connections, I suggest you start checking out just how good a citizen he really is. But there are exceptions to this rule.

Occasionally, an honest man is thrown into a situation where he can be of assistance. It's rare, but it happens. Even more rare is the good citizen who finds himself in this position and is not too frightened to get involved. (Remember that these people are not accustomed to dealing with the criminal element and assume that if they help you, they'll automatically wind up floating in the East River.) But if you happen to stumble across an informant who is clean, can help, and is willing to do so, by all means put him to work.

An older gentleman who was a friend of my father's once called me and said he'd found what he suspected was marijuana growing on some land he owned. A little investigation proved he was right—it wasn't ragweed, which is what these calls usually turn out to be about. Not only was marijuana growing on his property, there was lots of the old Mary Jane, which had been carefully cultivated. Officers set up on the field but never saw any activity, so the marijuana was destroyed.

This man is a good citizen. He wanted to help fight crime, life had afforded him the opportunity, and he had the courage to do so. Then he made sure that I didn't get a good night's sleep for two years by calling me every night with stories about how the Mafia was after him.

The Revenger. Informants whose motivation is vengeance come from both sides of the law. The majority, however, are criminals who have a bone to pick with another bad guy. They believe that if they can "do" (set up) their victim and chalk up a few brownie points with the cops at the same time, they've killed two birds with one stone. You should be aware of such setups when using criminal revenge informants.

I'm aware of one incident where the informant established his reliability through several small drug purchases, and then planted three pounds of marijuana beneath the back seat of his target's Volkswagen. He then provided evidence that the dope was there, and a search warrant was obtained. The object of his hatred was arrested, loudly protesting his innocence as he was cuffed and taken to jail. (But have you ever known a criminal who didn't?) The case had already been filed by the time the truth came out, which has to make you wonder if the truth sometimes doesn't come out. Granted, the owner of the Volkswagen was a drug dealer and deserved to spend a good deal of time "making little ones out of big ones," but not this way.

On the other hand, one of the strongest and most trustworthy informants I ever worked with was a revenge-motivated farmhand named Johnny. Johnny and his attractive young wife rented a small house from a farmer named Ned—for whom Johnny also worked. Ned harvested more than wheat and barley and ran a veritable pharmaceutical supply store out of his own house. He had a lot of money, and one of his hobbies was competing in tractor pulls. (For you city folk, this is a contest in which tractors are chained back-to-back and pulled against each other to see which one can drag the other over a line. Don't ask me, I don't know why either.)

His other hobby was sending Johnny off to fix fences at the far end of the pasture and then hurrying to the rental house and attempting to seduce Johnny's wife. Wife told husband. Husband told us. Johnny introduced me to Ned, I made several PCP buys from him, and Ned was arrested.

Revenge was sweet for Johnny. Johnny's wife was pleased as well. Ned's attorney became the owner of several of Ned's hot-rod tractors, which looked more like space shuttles than farm equipment. Ned was subjected to his own sexual harassment in the penitentiary, and I heard that the phrase "making little ones out of big ones" took on a whole new meaning for him.

The Convict Working Off a Case. For the most part, "rollovers" are the best informants you can get. These guys are criminals, and you should never trust them. They have been busted and face prison time unless you can convince the district attorney's office to drop the charges, or you can recommend a suspended sentence. Therefore, they want to see bad guys get busted, too. You each have a mutual goal—even if your motivations are different.

Experienced cons know this game at least as well as you do, and they are the hardest of all informants to control. They must be spoken to sternly at times (you may read between the lines here), for they will do everything in their power to play on both sides of the fence.

Cops like to say that they don't make deals with criminals, but this is nonsense; it happens every day, and any officer who is honest with himself knows it. The deal you are offering, in simple language, is this: if the informant helps you bust somebody who's a bigger criminal than they are for a bigger crime than they committed, you'll pass that information on to the prosecuting attorney. You are not guaranteeing a suspended or even a reduced sentence—only a judge can do that. Never promise an informant something that you can't back up, as word hits the streets faster than a $3 hooker, and you'll find future informants in short supply.

Normally, the crime you are holding over the head of this informant will need to be a felony or he will not consider working for you worth the risk. There are exceptions, however, such as someone whose parole or probation could be revoked for a misdemeanor, or a prominent person in the community whose reputation would suffer if word of an arrest leaked out. For years, Mark and I had a great relationship with some pharmaceutical students at a local university who got busted on misdemeanor drug possession charges. A misdemeanor would have prohibited them from being issued a license to practice pharmacy, and they were very willing to cooperate.

The Mercenary. This person becomes an informant primarily for money. To put it simply, you pay the mercenary to help you bust bad guys. Some "mercs" are good at their work, others are worthless. All must be watched like foxes in a henhouse.

If you pay the mercenary by the case, it means the more busts he makes, the more money he gets. If you give him a specific amount for a specific time like a salary, it means that doing a lot of cases during that period drives up his fee the next time you negotiate. It makes no difference which way you pay a mercenary—more arrests mean more money. Which, in turn, means there is strong incentive and temptation for the mercenary to set up innocent victims.

Mercenaries may work harder than any other type of informant you ever use, but remember why they're working so hard, and, like any other informant, never trust them completely.

These categories are not mutually exclusive of one another. For example, a mercenary may also want revenge on a specific target, and a good citizen might take money if it is offered. Regardless of what type of informant you use, make sure he understands the ground rules from the onset of the investigation. Some cases are far more dangerous than others, and if your informant is going to play with the big boys, he should start acting like one. Make sure your informant knows that you will hold him personally responsible if anything goes wrong and exactly what that entails. (You're reading between the lines again, I hope.)

Using Informants

You and your informant must get your story together before going on a case. You're Mickey Jordan from Atlanta and you and he are old army buddies, or you're his second cousin who deals hashish in Birmingham and you've come to town so he can help you find new connections. Whatever your story and reason to be there is, make it believable.

Interview your informant about who he knows and who he can do. Double-check everything he tells you with other sources. (Remember the training exercise in which we discussed the fact that people lie?) Then determine who your most likely targets are, and send your informant out to reestablish his connections.

The story your informant gives to the targeted dealer must include enough specifics to ensure authenticity. "I have a friend in town who wants some dope" won't hack it. Have a specific plan that includes a specific drug and a specific quantity. It can be altered later if need be; if you want heroin and all the dealer has is cocaine, it's better that you let him talk you into the coke.

If possible, establish telephone contact with the dealer yourself. Discuss whatever details he is willing to talk about over the phone (record the conversation if you work in a one-party consent state where both parties do not have to agree to a recording) and arrange to meet. Some dealers work out of their residences or offices, while others deal from cars or on the street. Depending on how dangerous you suspect your target is (remember that a cornered mouse can turn into a lion), you may want to arrange the first buy on ground that is neutral to both of you. The larger the deal, the more normal such a precaution will seem to the dealer. Remember that he is not only wondering if you are a cop, he is also wondering if you plan to rip him off. A $100,000 cocaine transaction warrants special security for both buyer and seller. On the other hand, treating the purchase of a $30 bag of grass as if it were some top-secret cloak-and-dagger operation will arouse suspicion.

Your informant will most likely go with you, at least to your first buy from the target he introduced you to, and he should be searched thoroughly for contraband ahead of time. If the informant is as well-acquainted with your mark as he claims, though this is often not the case, and there are no other unforeseen problems, the introduction should go well. But remember that no matter how comfortable the dealer may be acting, in the back of his mind he is still wondering if you are what you actually are—a cop.

PLANNING THE BUY

Before the deal goes down, you must decide whether you will "walk" after the buy or do a "buy/bust." If you're buying a small quantity of drugs and spending a small amount of money, you may wish to make several purchases from this dealer before busting him. This establishes a sales pattern and proves to any knee-jerk bleeding-heart liberals on the jury that the sale was not just a one-time "mistake" on the part of some poor, underprivileged victim of society. Multiple buys may also enable you to eventually "duke" the informant out of the transactions and buy from the dealer on your own. This, in theory, makes it less evident that your informant is the reason the dealer ends up behind bars, although I have found this to be more of a product of wishful thinking rather than reality. After an arrest, bad guys have a lot of time on their hands, and all they do is file lawsuits, rape each other, and try to figure out who got them busted.

If the buy is too large to walk away from, you will be arresting the dealer either at the scene or nearby. Make sure your surveillance and arrest team is in place, and plan the details of how and when the arrest will go down. If you are wearing a transmitter, establish a code word that will tell the other officers when it is time to move in. But remember that when transmitters and receivers malfunction, it is always at the worst times. Even though you are wired, you should have an alternate means of communication with your arrest team.

MAKING THE BUY

Right before you leave to make the buy, conduct a thorough search of yourself, your informant, your vehicle, and anything and anyone else that will be going with you. You should have nothing with you that could even remotely finger you as a cop.

I will never forget the feeling that overcame me one

night when I was sitting in a dealer's house with a rookie undercover officer. We were preparing to purchase a large quantity of amphetamines, and the dealer was busy with his scales. I happened to glance at the rookie officer's hand and noticed that he was wearing an FBI academy ring. I not only wanted to shoot him, I felt like putting the gun in my own mouth for not spotting it sooner. Luckily, I was able to get his attention and point out the problem without the bad guy noticing. The officer kept his hand in his pocket the rest of the night, and when we got back to the office, I had a long fatherly talk with him. He was new to the game, so I was as gentle as possible. I think all I threatened to do was cut his ring finger off if it ever happened again.

While you are doing the deal, remember to be simultaneously subjective and objective. Convince your target that you are who you say you are, but don't do it so well that you convince yourself. You must remain objective enough to mentally note significant details, such as pertinent times and dialogue.

There is only one constant when it comes to drug deals: there are no constants. No two drug deals are ever the same. There will always be something that will not go quite as you'd planned. It may be something big, or it may be something small, but somewhere along the line you will be thrown a monkey wrench that forces you to think on your feet and alter your strategy. But that's okay. You're an Explorer, remember? Improvisation is what you're good at.

CHAPTER 8

Robbery, Burglary, and Theft

The vast majority of burglaries and other thefts are investigated through traditional means. In other words, a crime is committed, discovered, and the police are notified. Investigators arrive at the scene, gather physical evidence, take statements, and write a report. This cycle usually begins again at the scene of another crime, with no one in jail for the previous one. Why is the percentage of unsolved crimes against property so high? There are two reasons.

First, regardless of whether they are city police detectives, county deputy sheriffs, or state or federal agents, investigators are almost always carrying a caseload larger than what any human being can be expected to manage successfully. So, in the same way wartime medics survey battlefields and quickly separate the soldiers who are injured beyond hope from those who still stand a chance of being saved, investigators learn to determine which cases have a reasonably good chance of being solved from those that don't.

Second, in a society like ours, crimes against property are

considered less important than crimes against people. Let's face it—murders, rapes, and aggravated assaults are more serious than somebody breaking into your house and stealing your precious TV while you were on vacation.

WORKING WITH "STRAIGHT" DETECTIVES

Experienced investigator's often know who committed a specific burglary, but they are unable to produce enough evidence to take the thief to court. This is one of the most frustrating situations in law enforcement. Most good criminals have a method of operation that they adhere to because it has worked for them in the past. To the cop who has seen a particular criminal's modus operandi before, it is almost as conclusively identifying as a fingerprint. I said *almost*.

I happened to be in a medium-sized sheriff's department one day when two deputies wheeled a safe into the evidence room. The safe had been opened by a method known as "peeling"—inserting a pry bar into the crack between the door and the frame and pounding it with a sledgehammer. I looked at the safe and said, "You know who did that?" in a tone of voice that told them that I knew.

"No, Jerry, we don't," a deputy I'll call Larry said sarcastically. "Why don't you tell us?"

I shrugged. "David Lassiter," I said. Lassiter (not his real name) was a skilled safe burglar from another part of the state, and it looked to me like he had expanded his territory.

Larry and the other deputy made a few sarcastic comments about my thinking I was Sherlock Holmes, but I stuck to my opinion—I'd seen David's work before. The discussion ended with a $10 bet that I was wrong.

The next day, I went back to the sheriff's office. Larry was triumphant. "You owe me ten," he gloated. "I checked and David Lassiter's in the penitentiary."

I paid him and chalked up my mistake to being a little overconfident in my ability to recognize tool marks. But about a month later, when I returned to the same sheriff's department, Larry approached me and handed me a $5 bill. "We got the safecracker," he said, "and I'd say you were half right."

I frowned.

"It was David Lassiter's nephew. The old man must have taught him the trade."

Particularly in small- to medium-sized cities, but to a certain extent in metropolitan areas as well, the police and bad guys are on a first-name basis. They know each other well, and each team knows how the other plays the game. For example, an investigator at the scene of a burglary may note that the glass was carefully cut out of a rear window using a glass cutter and 1-inch white adhesive tape, the fragments were swept up and removed, the rooms of the house were systematically worked from right to left, and the drawers were carefully closed again after being opened, and say to himself, "Yep, it's that anal-retentive burglar Ralph Breaksinsky again." The point is, the investigator knows exactly who committed the crime. But he has nothing so far that would be admissible in court. So, unless he can find a way to directly link the crime to good old Ralph, he can't arrest the man.

GATHERING INTELLIGENCE

So what does all this have to do with undercover work? I'm glad you asked. Basically, there are two ways to work burglaries and thefts in an undercover capacity. The first is, quite simply, by accident.

Accidents Happen

Regardless of what your main objective for going undercover may be, you will pick up little bits of unrelated criminal intelligence from time to time that may be significant to a case. Most of these fragments of information will go in one ear and out the other if they are not related to your primary goal, unless you take steps to ensure this does not happen.

Case in point: Very early in my career, I was sitting in the living room of two drug dealers I'll call "Darrel" and "Al." Darrel and Al were trying to decide whether or not I could be trusted to buy a hundred lot of white crosses. (Yes, I had gone in cold—I was too young and stupid to know better.) Anyway, Darrel, Al, and I drank Canadian whiskey for an hour or two, and then Darrel started telling me about what a great hustle a friend of his had going. I'll call the friend "Greg." Greg worked for the county's road construction crew, and every afternoon right before quitting time, he'd accidentally-on-purpose leave a few valuable tools hidden in the tall grass at the side of the road. (If you can't figure out the rest, you must be a Homesteader.)

To shorten the story, Greg made his surveillance video-tape debut a few afternoons later while hiding the tools. He did an encore performance that night when he returned to pick them up. We got search and arrest warrants, and in Greg's garage we found close to $50,000 worth of county equipment. But Greg had his fingers in other pies as well. In addition to the tools and other county property, he had stereos, televisions, guns, and other easily fenced items— all stolen, of course. After Greg got busted, his friends Darrel and Al didn't trust me. I never did get to buy that hundred lot of speed. A damn shame, wasn't it?

In other words, do not let little pearls of intelligence such as these escape you. Sometimes they will be lies or exaggerations and will lead nowhere. Other times, they will send you down a road far more important than the one you were plodding along. I have no doubt that Darrel and Al told me about Greg to see if he'd get busted. They want-ed to find out if I was a cop or an informant. Well, I took the bait, and they achieved their purpose. So what? They were nothing compared to Greg, and by now, some other under-cover officer has undoubtedly opened the penitentiary door for them anyway.

Sometimes, you may choose to act on these extraneous yet valuable fragments of intelligence yourself. Other

Keep an open mind—small crimes sometimes open the door to bigger busts. These stolen weapons, and close to $100,000 worth of other stolen property, were netted through a search warrant that was issued as a result of a small amphetamine buy. (Photo by Ed Porter)

times, you will want to pass them on to straight investigators (those who are not undercover) who can follow up on them. If you are worried about preserving your anonymity, develop a relationship with a straight cop who you trust. It doesn't matter if he's a patrolman, traffic officer, detective, or even a midmanagement Homesteader; he can act as a go-between, and the investigators need never know where the intel came from. (On second thought, make sure he's a Homesteader. Those guys should be put to some kind of constructive use besides just shuffling paper.)

Targeting Known Criminals

The second method of working burglaries and thefts is to target a known criminal. This type of investigation is usually initiated in reverse order from those that are discovered by accident. For example, Detective Snurd, who worked on the Ralph Breaksinsky burglary earlier, comes to you with his intelligence: "Harvey, I know it's Breaksinsky," he says. "He's hit five houses in the last six weeks, all within a seven-block radius of where he's shacked up with that old whore of his. They all had evidence of the tape-and-cutter routine Ralph always uses, and the son-of-a-bitch still closes the drawers when he's finished looking through them. But he's smart. I've got nothing."

Put Informants to Work

The first thing you should do is round up your informants, separately—you don't want any of them knowing the others are working for you. Find out if any of them know Ralph the anal-retentive burglar. If so, great. His assignment is to reestablish his relationship with Ralph with an eye toward introducing you to Ralph somewhere down the line. You then become Ralph's best buddy and hope you can do one or more of the following:

1) Gather physical evidence of Ralph's little capers.
2) Learn about a job Ralph has planned and arrange for the boys in the blue suits to be waiting for him.

The theft of oil, oil field equipment, and property of all types is worked similarly to drug deals. Get an introduction by an informant before you decide how to set up your deal. (Photo by Jim Cash)

3) Work yourself into Ralph's confidence until you can accompany him on one of the burglaries.

If none of your informants know Ralph directly, try to determine if the orderly little thief and one of your informants have a mutual acquaintance that could be used. This adds an additional step to the investigation, but once a connection is made, you can pick up where you left off.

But if no connections can be made, pick the informant who has the most in common with Ralph and send him out to see if he can get to know Ralph. Yes, that's going in cold, but the informant is more likely to pull it off than you are—he's a certified crust deposit and has a street rep to prove it, while you're a new face with no bona fide rabble credentials. Besides, it's better to waste his time than yours. When you tell your informant to do this, he's going to act like you just ordered him to walk a tightwire over Niagara Falls carrying a rabid Doberman pinscher under each arm. So you will have to remind him that he's still facing 5 to 10 years on those PCP charges—at the same correctional facility as the bad guys against whom he's already testified.

Assisting a Burglary

Let's say that you have gained enough of Ralph's confidence that he decides he wants you as a partner on his next job. Be careful. You are about to enter one of the most physically and politically dangerous areas of undercover work, and law enforcement for that matter.

There are certain things you must do before the burglary goes down:

1) Make sure the straight officers know what's going on, and give yourself time to set up surveillance on the site. If the exact site of the burglary is not known, you must designate a place where your surveillance team can pick you up, making sure there are an adequate number of vehicles allotted to provide an effective "tail."

2) Make sure every other cop who's going to be in on

the deal has a detailed physical description of you, including what you'll be wearing. (If possible, you should meet each officer ahead of time.)

3) You and the other officers should know whether Ralph carries a weapon during the commission of his crimes and what kind of weapon it is. If this cannot be ascertained in advance, assume that he is armed and that he won't hesitate to use his weapon.

These three steps are designed to protect both your rear end and your pension. But there are other decisions that must also be made:

1) Determine whether Ralph is to be arrested during the commission of the crime or after leaving the scene.

2) Decide if you will "turn cop" and assist with the arrest or remain undercover and "go down with the bust" in order to remain in Ralph's confidence.

It gets trickier. What kind of place is Ralph going to burglarize? If it's a residence, will the occupants be home? If so, you may consider arresting Ralph before he can enter the house, limiting your charges to attempted burglary or conspiracy to burglarize. Otherwise the lives of innocent people may be at great risk. If the residence will be empty, the owner should be informed ahead of time and his cooperation requested. Most citizens are more than willing to comply when they realize that they have been targeted and to refuse means that Ralph will come anyway—when the police are not waiting.

The police working in the area who are not part of the surveillance or arrest team must be alerted and asked to steer clear of the area. The location of the house should be given to the 911 dispatcher in case one of the neighbors calls when he sees you and Ralph break into the house. This brings up another question: does Ralph carry a police scanner with him like many burglars do? If he does, another can of worms is opened and you'll have to take special precautions to work around it.

The illusion of a burglary can be created with the help of a local merchant or homeowner. Beware the physical and legal traps and be ready to reimburse the helpful citizen for damages and/or loss. (Photo by Catherine Johnson)

There are perhaps a hundred more questions that must be answered before you assist in the commission of a crime, which is exactly what you are doing. Each situation is unique, so you should continually ask yourself, "What else could trip me up?" and "What else could endanger innocent bystanders?" You are walking a very fine line between doing your job and committing a felony, so prepare for every possible twist and turn.

Ralph the anal-retentive burglar wasn't invented to serve merely as an example. I once accompanied a burglar on a residential job who was every bit as fastidious as Ralph. The intended victims were out of town, my cohort did not use a police scanner, and everything went like clockwork—until we got in the house and found out that the homeowners had their own scanner, which they had left on. The first transmission we heard was some cop informing another, "the undercover officer is inside." But for all of his orderliness, Ralph wasn't all that smart. We listened to the radio traffic for 15 minutes while we worked the house, and he didn't catch on to the fact that the boys in blue were right outside until they broke in to arrest him.

Assisting an Armed Robbery

Of all thefts, armed robbery is perhaps the most dangerous to innocent bystanders. Before you decide to join Ralph's mean brother Spike and knock off a bank or convenience store, ask yourself about a thousand more questions than you did before doing the burglary. For instance, "What are you going to tell the family of the bank teller who gets shot by one of Spike's stray rounds?" and, "What are you going to tell the family of the bank teller who gets shot by one of *your* stray rounds?" Innocent people can get shot, even if you're posing as one of the tellers instead of working with Spike.

In most cases, armed robbery is a crime better left to more traditional forms of investigation. On the other hand, suppose you hear that a robbery is going to go down at the Friendly Farmer National Bank in 15 minutes, but you have no description of the perpetrators or their vehicle. What are you going to do, send a militia of blue suits to the Friendly Farmer National Bank, prompting the bad guys to drive down the street and make a hit on the Friendly Merchant Bank instead? No, you send your smartest, most levelheaded undercover cops, who are also members of the Governor's Pistol Team, to pose as customers or bank personnel, and then you pray that the god that watches over drunks and undercover officers is in a good mood. Armed robberies have been and will continue to be stopped by undercover officers, but this is not always possible, and it should be attempted only when there appears to be no better way of handling the situation.

SHOPLIFTING AND EMPLOYEE THEFT

Shoplifting and employee theft may be investigated by police, but preventing these crimes usually falls upon the shoulders of private security officers.

Shoplifters

Although the men and women in the light blue uniforms you see at Wal-Mart and Toys-R-Us serve a valuable purpose, when it comes to what the stores term as "mysterious disappearances of merchandise," a good "rent-a-cop" who understands undercover work is worth 50 officers wearing exposed badges.

The undercover security officer working shoplifters should enter the store posing as a shopper and behave just like any other customer. He should appear to be doing some serious shopping, going about his business and not making eye contact with anyone he suspects is stealing. (There's a reason God gave you peripheral vision.)

Shoplifters often work in pairs or groups. Here two teenagers are distracting the salesman and another is standing guard as the fourth slips merchandise down the front of his pants. The baggy styles currently in vogue are perfect for concealment. (Photo by Edward Hasbrook)

In some situations, the undercover security officer may find it beneficial to "accidentally" let a suspect see him secreting merchandise. Taking a nervous glance around the immediate area, and then stuffing a videotape under your coat will mark you as a rank amateur to an experienced thief, which may bring down the shoplifter's guard. Do not, however, attempt to form a "bond of comradery" with a suspected shoplifter. In other words, don't give him an "ah-so-we're-brothers smile" as you tuck a compact disk into your underwear. If the suspect is worth spending time on, it's because he's stealing a lot, which means he's an experienced thief. Experienced thieves aren't stupid, and they have no desire to be your friend or partner. They want to do their business and get out of there as fast as they can. If they pay attention to you at all, it's because they suspect that you are exactly what you are—the heat. Your job is to convince them that you're just some bumbling idiot trying to hoist a few cans of corned beef hash or whatever.

Thieving Employees

Employee theft is a little different. An employee who is stealing from his employer has certain advantages, the least of which is that he can usually cover carrying items outside the store with any of a number of pretexts: loading and unloading, inventory transfer to other stores, and so on. If you've been called in to work a store, chances are that the management already suspects one or more employees. And guess what? Nine times out of ten, they're right.

Before you begin, sit down with the store representative who called you in and determine exactly what he knows and how he knows it. If he only knows that 16 lawn mowers have disappeared in the last three months, and that Joe Fingers in the lawn and garden department has a dishonest face, you're starting from ground zero. Study carefully the company's personnel file on Joe, and gather all the other information about him that you can without alerting him to the fact that he's under investigation. Once this has been done, you'll start posing as a store employee, but not in the lawn and garden department. If they stick you with Joe right away and he's guilty, his radar antennae are going to start vibrating with 220 volts of power.

Take your time. Don't push things. Let Joe get used to seeing you around the store in your new uniform with the name tag on it. After you've been an employee awhile, you can be transferred to the lawn and garden department, and then you can keep an eye on Mr. Fingers. Perhaps some night he'll need help loading the mowers. If not, you'll at least begin to see things. Be sure to document the times that suspicious things happen, the serial numbers of the equipment involved, and any other pertinent information.

The ideal situation is to have an informant in the store. If the store rep tells you it wasn't just Joe Fingers' dishonest face that brought him to his attention, but that Freddy Screwdriver from the hardware department reported him, you're ahead in the game. Get Freddy in the office and find out firsthand what he knows, how he knows it, and how much help he's willing to offer. Be wary of Freddy's motives though, just as you would any other informant's: Why is he doing this? Is he an honest employee who doesn't like thieves, or does he have his own agenda? Was he in on the thefts, got scared, and decided to blame it all on Fingers before he got caught? How does he feel about Joe Fingers personally? If Freddy has something against Joe, how much of his story sounds true and how much sounds like he just wants to see his enemy fired or arrested? Also, how much of what Freddy tells you is from direct knowledge and how much is conjecture? Freddy may be trying to score career-advancement brownie points also, in which case he is sort of a "corporate" mercenary informant and should be watched as closely as any other merc.

After you've evaluated Freddy, have the manager place you in one of the departments close to the lawn and garden department, but not in Freddy's hardware area. If you do that, Freddy will be sidling up to you all day with conspiratorial looks and whispered bits of intelligence that mean nothing. Sooner or later, Joe Fingers will notice and suspect you.

There are other angles you can take. If Freddy was a party to the thefts before getting scared and informing, and you learn this before you appear in the store as an employee, he may be able to tell Joe Fingers that he knows a guy who'll pay more for the mowers than the fence they've been using. You then become the new fence. Even if you're already working the floor when you figure out that Freddy is dirty too, you may be able to get to know Joe well enough—probably through Freddy—to pull this off using another undercover officer posing as your friend and fence.

When using undercover work in the investigation of any form of stealing, be it robbery, burglary, or fraud, remember that no two cases are identical. Each offense has its own structure, good and bad guys, and little subtleties that make it stand apart from other situations. Each one must be played differently, and you must form your plan of attack ahead of time but be willing to deviate from that blueprint when the case inevitably throws you curves.

In forming your scheme, include the necessary details to create the illusion that you are truly what you profess to be: an employee, customer, or store accountant. Be creative in your planning, but never be overly dramatic for the sake of drama itself. Make full use of your imagination; it's your only limitation when working undercover.

CHAPTER 9

Homicide

As with theft, there are two ways to use undercover work when investigating homicides. They are: 1) before the fact, and 2) after the fact. I will consider them in reverse order.

POST-MURDER INVESTIGATIONS

Murder is usually one of the easiest crimes to solve. Most of the time, there's an obvious motive, physical evidence, and sometimes eyewitnesses. These can lead to a suspect who is more often than not a family member or acquaintance of the victim, and he's in jail within 24 hours of the discovery of the crime. Quite often, the suspect even confesses. This is the norm.

It's the abnormal murders—the exceptions to this rule—that attract the public's interest. These murders spawn novels, movies, and television shows, but they can cause homicide investigators to pull their hair out by the roots, become alcoholics, or stick their guns in their mouths and pull the trigger.

There's an old maxim among cops that if you don't crack a murder case during the first 24 hours after it occurred, the odds against solving it increase dramatically. This is all too true. Homicide investigations usually fall into one of two categories: real easy or real hard. Very few are in between. Obviously, the easy murder cases don't call for much undercover work. They don't call for much work at all—that's why they're called "easy."

The homicide cases in which undercover work is often used to good advantage are those where you don't have much to begin with. These are the murders that may have an abundance of physical evidence, and even witnesses, but the invaluable key to both, motive, is missing. In other words, there's nothing to link the evidence at the crime scene to the person who perpetrated the crime, and undercover work becomes sort of a last resort. But considering the importance we place on the unlawful taking of another person's life, it is worth giving it a try.

Regardless of whether the investigation is simple or difficult, if the suspect has not confessed, try planting an undercover officer in the cell next to him. True, your suspect has probably seen this ploy in countless movies and TV shows, but who knows? He may have a weak moment and start talking. In any case, what do you have to lose?

Consulting Informants

First, as always, go to your informants. Any good cop can tell you that if word on the streets is traveling, it is traveling fast. But just as an undercover narcotics officer is tempted to ignore bits of intelligence concerning a theft, your drug informants may assume that you are interested only in drug cases. So ask them directly, "Do you know anything about Rob Howard's murder?" Sometimes, you get lucky.

Suppose, however, that the god of undercover officers

is not smiling on you today, and you don't get an answer like, "Rob Howard? Sure. Cary Gamble shot him and the gun's in Cary's underwear drawer." Still, your informant may know something that, when linked to what the homicide investigators know, proves valuable. Interview the informant thoroughly. What you are looking for is an underworld rumor.

The world's biggest gossips are school teachers, cops, and criminals. Which of these professions deserves the number one ranking is up for grabs, but the bad guys certainly do their share of rumor mongering. And, like all hearsay, a criminal rumor may or may not be true. The most likely case—as with all gossip—is that the story has some basis in fact but was distorted in its telling and retelling.

So far you haven't done anything the straight investigators haven't done, you've just done it with a different set of informants—yours. But let's assume that Harry Best, your numero uno informant, tells you that the word on the streets is that Rob Howard was blackmailing some bartender who was having an extramarital affair. That's all Best knows. The reason that's all he knows is that he wasn't particularly interested until now. So it's time for you to spark some of his interest by telling him that if he doesn't find out more, he's going back to the penitentiary, or he's not getting paid, or whatever else applies to his case. Send him back to the streets to learn more. Remember, he can gather intel faster than you can.

Let's assume (forget that old ass-u-me thing for the time being) that Harry Best comes back and tells you that Rob Howard spent a lot of time at the Friendly Bar & Grill on the corner of 36th and Maple. And he also found out that the bartender is married, but he hasn't heard anything about the man having an affair. It's time for you to put on your best beer drinking hat and go find a dark table in the corner of the Friendly Bar & Grill. Although you are not known as a cop there, you might as well take your informant with you for extra cover.

Going Undercover

Drink beer, shoot some pool, and have some fun, but at the same time, keep a watchful eye on the bartender. You are watching to see if he makes goo-goo eyes at the short-skirted barmaid, or gets phone calls 10 times a day and talks at the pay phone in the corner with a hushed voice. You may see him glance furtively at the female mail carrier when she hands the mail across the bar, or at the lady who drives the Budweiser truck when she makes her delivery. But remember that society is not the same as it was 20 years ago, so don't automatically discount the guy in the UPS uniform who swishes in with a package under his arm.

To put it simply, look for all the same things the homicide investigators do, but approach the case from a different angle—an undercover angle. Present yourself as nothing more than a beer-drinking, eight-ball shooting customer, and if you do it convincingly, you will circumvent the bartender's automatic defenses that would have been generated by the badge-flashing straight detective.

You spend three afternoons in the Friendly Bar & Grill, and not only does the bartender not appear to have a girlfriend, you're questioning whether the old white-haired fart even has a life away from the bar. You never thought you'd get sick of beer, but you're well on your way. You're one step away from deciding this whole idea was a crock and wondering if it's time you got back to work on those eunuch transvestite prostitutes who sell barbiturates. (Well, maybe you have time for a couple more beers first.)

Suddenly, a guy wearing polyester slacks and a shirt unbuttoned to his navel walks in, acting like he owns the place—because he does—and disappears into the office with the short-skirted barmaid. Remember what I said about rumors being based on fact but getting distorted through their telling and retelling? Here is an alternate scenario: Rob Howard was blackmailing the bar *owner*, not the bar*tender*. You go back and tell the detective in charge of Rob Howard's homicide. He jumps up and down and urinates in his pants because this is the one bit of missing information that ties all the other leads together. Suddenly, Winston Foolaround, the owner of the Friendly Bar & Grill, is in jail awaiting trial for Rob Howard's murder.

Congratulations. Winnie was charged because you did good work. You used your imagination and undercover work in a way that is often overlooked. Was it a long shot? Yes, but this example was based on a real homicide that was solved exactly in this manner. Sometimes long shots pay off—ask anyone who's won a lottery or picked an unlikely winner at the Preakness. If an investigation hits a dead end, you've got nothing to lose by giving the negative odds a try. And if you want to kill two birds with one stone, make a few drug buys through your informant while the two of you are drinking beer at the Friendly Bar & Grill.

PRE-MURDER INVESTIGATIONS

Working a homicide from an undercover angle after the murder has been committed always has and always will yield fewer results than working a homicide before it occurs. A post-murder undercover investigation ending with convicting the killer is indeed a long shot, but a pre-murder investigation has great chances of putting a bad guy behind bars for a long time. Even if you bungle the deal, you at least keep the intended victim from getting killed and alert him to the fact that he's been targeted. This will make you feel good, and it will make the murder target feel even better.

But, ladies and gentlemen, there is another aspect to working before-the-fact homicides from an undercover perspective that should not go unheralded. Quite simply, it's the most fun you can have with your clothes on. Put on your beard, and then go out and buy all the dope and stolen property you can find; catch so many thieves that the mayor gives you the key to the city and the local Neighborhood Watch Program invites you to speak at their meetings; go undercover as an office employee and bust some pencil-necked accountant who was embezzling a million dollars a day; or solve a murder like Rob Howard's after the fact—but you still won't have as much fun as you will playing a real, live hit man, which is exactly what you will do when you hear that someone is looking for a contract triggerman. You will step into the part of the hired killer and agree to do the killing for a set price.

The Undercover Hit Man

Murder-for-hire is not as rare as most people think, nor is it relegated only to organized crime. Both men and women search for paid killers every day for a variety of reasons: a drug dealer gets ripped off on a deal and wants revenge, a legitimate businessman wants his partner out of the way, husbands want their wives dead, wives want their husbands dead. But most people don't want to pull the trigger themselves.

Here's an imaginary but typical scenario of how these things usually go down. Don Black decides that Earth would be a better planet with his wife, Sharon, residing six feet below it. Maybe he wants to collect on Sharon's life insurance policies, or maybe he caught Sharon fooling around and decided nothing but her death could pacify his broken heart. There could be a hundred other reasons he wants Sharon dead, but for whatever reason, Don's decided his wife needs to die.

The truth is Don has a girlfriend who he wants to marry. He owns a large automobile dealership in a major city and fears a divorce might leave Sharon in control of his company. So he decides murder is his only option, but he doesn't want to get his own hands dirty. Don isn't the type of citizen who is on a first-name basis with any *la cosa nostra* triggermen, the Crips and Bloods don't come over to his house for Friday night bridge parties, and he can't remember the last time he had a drink with any member of the Manson family. In other words, Don doesn't have any good criminal connections.

So what does a man in Don's situation do? He goes to

the seediest guy he knows—a guy from a dark corner of his life who may be a convicted felon, or who, rumor has it, is a bookmaker for organized crime, or who, at the very least, has a reputation for being less than honest in some way. In Don's case, this turns out to be one of his used car salesmen, Jimmy. You see, until he began contemplating murder, Don's biggest crime was that he never quite grew out of the 1960s; he scores an ounce bag of marijuana from Jimmy every month or so, and while he knows that Jimmy is no hit man, he is the closest person to a real, live bad guy Don knows. So Don takes Jimmy out for a beer after work one night and tells him what he needs.

Jimmy's just a small-time dope dealer and probably doesn't know where to start looking for hired killers. Hit men don't advertise in the Yellow Pages or under the situations wanted section in the classifieds, and I've never heard of one buying a radio or television spot to advertise his services. Jimmy can't help Don, but he sees a way to make Don's situation work for himself. Unbeknownst to Don, Jimmy sold you a gram of coke two months earlier, and he's been trying to work off this mistake ever since. So he comes to you with the story.

As I said earlier, get ready for some fun.

Meeting the Client

After Jimmy tells you all he knows, and you learn everything else you can about Don and Sharon, send Jimmy back to his employer with the story that he's found a guy who can do the job, and have him set up a meeting between you (posing as the hit man) and Don. Don may balk at this idea, preferring to work through Jimmy instead, but do your best to prevent this from happening. The case will be much stronger if you can tell the jury that Don asked you face-to-face to kill his wife. Add to this testimony a tape recording of Don making his request, the money he pays you, and the other evidence you pick up along the way, and Don will be on his way to a place where he can meet real, live murderers.

When playing the part of hit man, the initial interview may take place anywhere. Here a disgruntled husband is contracting the murder of his wife. (Photo by Edward Hasbrook)

But how adamant should you be about meeting with Don? What if he flat refuses? Remember, you are dealing with a man who has made up his mind that he wants his wife dead, and he's already taken steps to find somebody who'll do the job for him. All of this took place over a period of days, and that means Don didn't just get mad at his wife and make a drunken statement like, "I oughta get somebody to kill the bitch," that got blown out of proportion. If you're too inflexible, he's going to find someone else to do the job, and the next person he hires may be a real hit man and may not care whether he meets Don face-to-face or not.

A decent case can still be made with only a recorded telephone conversation between you and Don. (I'm assuming you live in a one-party consent state.) Or, depending upon how much you trust Jimmy and how reliable you think he will appear to a jury, you may want him to wear a recorder or transmitter and arrange the hit through him.

Let's say that Don agrees to meet you, and you're waiting for him at a local Burger King wearing your favorite safari jacket. Your hair falls to your shoulders, your beard is unkempt, you're doing that crazy little twitch you do with one eye, and you look like the burned-out, Vietnam-era, U.S. Marine Corps sniper-turned-hippie that is part of your identity when you go undercover as a hit man.

Don walks in. You wave him over, and he sits down. You can growl, talk in a low, menacing voice, exaggerate the tick, eat broken glass, or put cigarette butts out in the palm of your hand, but you don't have to do any of this. Nothing you do is going to change the way Don already feels about you, because what Don sees across the table from him is not a real-life hit man, but the manifestation of a Hollywood image he's been watching on the big screen since he was a kid. And Don is probably about to defecate in his boxers.

Don's voice will reflect his fear, so if you're recording the conversation (audio, video, or both), you need to make sure that it is clear that killing Sharon is his idea, not yours. Give him every chance to change his mind, and make him feel as comfortable with you as possible. Even if you don't record, you will have to testify later as to what was said, and you can rest assured that Don's attorney is going to try to make it look like Don didn't really want to put a contract on his wife but he was afraid to say no to big bad you.

Establish a Price and Proof

You and Don will have to agree on a price. Before meeting with Don, you should have a fairly good idea of how much he is able and willing to pay. Get the most money from him that you can, as though you were doing the job for real. This does not mean you can't negotiate, but if you agree to work too cheaply, Don will suspect that something is amiss. You are walking a fine line here, because you don't want Don to say no to you and then shop around for a bargain basement hit.

Once the price is agreed upon, you should demand some

of the money up front. Fifty percent is standard in the trade, with the other half to be paid when proof is provided that the murder was carried out. And what is that proof to be? Again, you and Don will have to decide. It may be the victim's bill-fold, wedding ring, or perhaps her bloody shirt or jacket. A rule of thumb is, never agree to provide something you cannot actually produce. Problems sometimes arise at this point, and you will have to be creative and think fast.

I once "contracted" with an extremely vicious wife who wanted to have her husband killed. She not only demanded his wedding ring, she wanted me to cut off his ring finger and bring it along, too. I had to use my "I'm-even-crazier-than-you" act and say, "Look, bitch, I don't play these games. You want me to cut off a finger? Hell, I'll just cut off his fuckin' head and bring it to you." We settled on his wedding ring and a few other personal items that he carried. Ain't love grand?

In another case, a husband caught his wife having an affair and not only wanted her done in, he wanted me to rape her first and videotape the whole thing. I told him in no uncertain terms that I was not a rapist. (Such twisted rationalizations—"I'll murder, but I won't rape"—are not all that uncommon among hard-core criminals.) I then went on to tell him that I found his idea highly offensive, and that if he ever suggested such a thing again, I would consider raping and killing him. This was a bizarre and off-the-wall threat, but it got his attention, and he settled for his wife's purse and wig. Remember your ace in the hole when dealing with people like this: they are very frightened of you and don't want you to get mad at them. But also remember that there are exceptions.

The "Murder" Plan

Don will want to know how you plan to kill his wife. Tell him that you don't know yet; it will depend on several variables. Ask questions about Sharon's personal life and leave the impression that you are formulating a plan. Don't tell him exactly what the plan is—let him think he pieced it together himself. Before you leave, make arrangements to meet with Don after the hit has been carried out, then take your 50-percent down payment, mark it as evidence, and go see Sharon.

Contacting the Murder Target

When talking to Sharon, keep in mind that you may well be "bursting her balloon." She may have thought that she and Don were living a life of mutual adoration, similar to that usually reserved for Harlequin Romance novels. You and at least one other officer (preferably female) should corner her somewhere away from Don, identify yourselves, and make her aware of the little surprise he is planning. Be prepared for her reaction, which may be anything from, "I knew that bastard had someone on the side!" to total disbelief. If she refuses to face reality, use your recorded conversations with Don to convince her.

Explain to Sharon that what Don has done is called conspiracy to commit murder, and that you need her help in gathering the evidence that can put him away. If she refuses, explain that conspiracy to commit murder is what people do as a prelude to actual murder, and that if she does not put Don behind bars, he is likely to find a real killer. (It's amazing how quickly unreceptive intended victims agree to assist you once they fully understand this concept.)

Sharon should probably not go home again after you talk to her. You are dealing with a man who is intent on seeing her dead, and although it appears that Don doesn't intend to murder her himself, you can't be certain that he will not crack and change his mind. What is even more likely is that Sharon will somehow give the scheme away. Think about it. If you found out that your wife or husband was planning to have you killed, could you go home, sit down to dinner, and say, "Hey, how about those Dallas Cowboys, huh?"

"Doing the Hit" and Gathering Proof

How you proceed from this point depends on the details of what you and Don worked out. But, for the purposes of this example, let's assume that Don agrees to meet you at his lakeside cabin two days later, and that you will bring Sharon's driver's license, Sharon's wedding ring, and some evidence of how she was killed.

Get Sharon's wedding ring and driver's license from her, and in this particular case, I would be tempted to take her blouse, jacket, or other item of clothing that covers a vital area, hang it up, shoot it with a shotgun, rifle, or pistol, and cover it with animal blood or a blood substitute. (Animal blood can be obtained from a local slaughterhouse or stock yard. Blood substitutes that are realistic enough for this purpose can be made by mixing ketchup and other ingredients.)

In addition to the items of proof that Don demanded,

Creating the illusion of a "hit" can be done in a variety of ways. Here an officer is firing a shotgun into the back of the proposed victim's shirt. A little fake blood and a few photographs combined with watches, rings, or other personal items, and you're in business. (Photo by Gary Campbell)

The deed is done. Animal blood or ketchup-based mixtures are excellent blood substitutes for photographs. In this shot, we used chocolate syrup, which is easy to obtain and works well in black and white photographs. (Photo by Edward Hasbrook)

you may wish to provide a few Polaroid snapshots of Sharon's "dead" body. Dress Sharon in the blouse or other article that was shot and soiled, have her lie down and play dead, and photograph her. Remember that if she was shot in the chest, there will be blood on other areas of her body such as her face. (This is where the ketchup mixture comes in handy—few women, or men for that matter, relish the idea of having their faces painted with pig's blood.)

Providing Proof, Collecting Money, and Making the Arrest

When you are finished "doing the hit," go to the cabin to meet with Don and trade the evidence that you killed his wife for the rest of your fee. If possible, this meeting should be recorded. Keep in mind that Don owns an automobile dealership and isn't used to dealing with hit men, and he's going to be very nervous at this meeting. Make sure that your final performance is every bit as convincing as the one you gave at Burger King; you are gathering the evidence that will convince the jury beyond a reasonable doubt that this was not just some sick joke on Don's part—he fully intended to turn his living, breathing spouse into a corpse.

Remember this: no matter how big of a "puss" Don has appeared to be so far, the thought of killing you has been going through his mind. Here's where Don's TV training comes in again (and by TV I don't mean transvestite). Don has seen countless murder-for-hire plots on the screen, and in at least half of them, the guy who hired the hit man subsequently took out the killer so there wouldn't be any witnesses. Don has also been thinking about the new life that's ahead of him with a new woman, and he doesn't intend to miss it getting raped in prison. He may decide that he should kill you to ensure that his new Shangri-la all comes about.

Prepare for this possibility before you arrive at Don's lakeside hideaway. This means making sure whatever weapons you carry are readily accessible, but more importantly it means readying your mind to defend yourself if it becomes necessary. Recognize and come to terms with the fact that you may have to kill Don.

Your backup team will be at the lake, but its primary objective will be to pull surveillance. As I have already stressed, it is unlikely that it will arrive in time to help if Don tries to kill you. The backup team members can be positioned on the lake fishing in boats, water skiing, or whatever else looks natural. But remember that their main reason to be there is to be able to testify later—not protect you. Your safety is your responsibility.

You must decide whether you will arrest Don at the lake, which may or may not be a good idea. Don will be under a lot of stress at that point, and there is always a chance that the sudden sight of a badge will push him over the edge. If he does turn into a screaming yellow zonker and pulls an Uzi from under the couch, at least there is less chance that harm will come to innocent citizens in such an isolated setting.

On the other hand, it might be wise to let Don think he's pulled off the crime of the century, take the rest of the hit money, and just leave, planning to arrest him later. Don only wanted his wife out of the picture—he won't be a danger to anyone else during this interlude (that includes you, because as any good hit man would do, you did not furnish Don with any way of locating you). So, the next morning when Don is sitting smugly behind his desk and is far more relaxed (read that "less likely to have a gun handy"), you and a few other men in blue can walk in and slap the cuffs on him.

Debriefing

Once the evidence of the hit and the money changes hands, it's over. You'll either drive back to town with Don in tow or wait to arrest him later. In either case, Don is going to jail, poor Sharon is going to start putting the pieces of her crumbled life back together, and you and everyone else who had a part in the case will head for the nearest cop bar to down a few and tell yourselves how wonderful you are. You'll discuss the case, looking at the things that went right, the things that went wrong, and the things that could have gone wrong but didn't. At some point during this celebration, take a little time to ask yourselves why the undercover operation was successful. I can give you the answer ahead of time if you like—it's because you planned well. You had every detail you could think of under control before you went undercover, which afforded you the ability to concentrate on things occurring that you hadn't anticipated after you "put on your beard."

An undercover operation is like a chess game with distorted, ever-changing rules. As in chess, you go into the game with a plan, but you must be willing to modify that plan each time your opponent makes a move you hadn't counted on. That's called strategy, and I'm going to take a look at it in detail next.

PART 4

STRATEGY

CHAPTER 10
Electronic Aids

This chapter is not about a disease that your microwave oven can acquire through loose sexual behavior or by sharing intravenous needles. It's about the use of transmitters, receivers, and audio and video recorders in undercover work.

First, let me make it clear that I do not profess to be an electronics expert. The depth of my understanding of how recorders, transmitters, and receivers function might be likened to the fact that I know punching the correct buttons on my television's remote control will enable me to watch *Seinfeld* on Thursday nights. Do not mistake what I am saying, though. Ignorance in this, or any other area of police work that surrounds your undercover chores, is nothing to be proud of. The more you know about the individual parts of an undercover operation that work together to make felony cases (undercover officers, surveillance teams, listening posts, and equipment), the better off you will be.

I know and understand only the bare essentials concerning the field of electronics in law enforcement (007 was my hero as a kid, not Q). For the most part, how bugs work is as much a mystery to me as how that assortment of contraptions beneath the hood of my Chevy Blazer makes it travel down the street. But I know how to drive my car, and I know how to use tape recorders and transmitters during undercover operations. More importantly, I know how to head off the equipment problems that can arise to ruin otherwise solid cases.

If you are an electronics buff, you know all these things and more. If you aren't, don't let those enigmatic wires and plugs intimidate you. You may not know exactly how the gas pump in your car gets the gasoline into the engine, but you do know that if you let the little red needle on the gas gauge drop down to the big E, the engine will cough a few times and stop running. Likewise, if you're undercover wearing a Bell & Howell 1/4-watt transmitter and the battery exhausts its charge, you know that your surveillance team won't be able to listen to you anymore.

I'll take a practical approach when discussing the use of electronic surveillance equipment undercover, since the actual function of these devices does not fall within the scope of this book. If you are interested in learning more, and I stress that the more you know about every area that surrounds your undercover role the better, there are a multitude of good texts on the subject.

A NECESSARY EVIL

When I began working undercover, the use of electronic devices was rare and primarily limited to federal agencies, a few states, and larger police and sheriff's departments. In fact, my partner and I made hundreds of successful felony cases without burning up so much as one 9-volt battery. This meant that we had fewer peripheral details to worry about, which allowed us to concentrate on our undercover performances more, and, in spite of what some Homesteaders will tell you, we were in far less danger of bodily harm going "naked" (without electronic devices). Like Dana Carvey's grumpy old man character used to say on *Saturday Night Live*, "That's the way it was, and we liked it."

I still prefer working without body mikes and recorders. Unfortunately, they are a necessary evil these days. You used to be able to put on your beard, buy some drugs or do whatever other deal you were involved in, arrest the criminal, and have a judge and jury take your word over his because you are a police officer and he is slime that can miraculously walk and talk. But American society's moral standards and ideas concerning right and wrong have changed over the last two decades, and recently that change has been rapid. Lying now seems to be expected of public officials (look who's in the White House). Since many citizens view the police as an extension of the government, and they know little about the unique psychological make-up of police officers and their fervent desire to see justice prevail, they assume that all police officers lie as loudly as politicians. Add to this the fact that the very few dishonest officers there are get 99 percent of the publicity, and . . . well, I think you get my drift.

Much of what was considered wrong 20 years ago is now considered right, and shame on you if you don't jump in line and behave in a politically correct manner. The "good old days" are gone, at least temporarily, and all the bitching and moaning in the world isn't going to change that. The bottom line is, a police officer is not as likely to be taken at his word as he used to be. So you can't just tell the judge and jury what happened anymore. Sometimes, you have to show them. Enter electronic surveillance and recording.

MONITORING AND RECORDING DEVICES

Now that that's off my chest, I will talk about putting these magic little devices to use catching and convicting

Recorders need not be expensive. Here Kay County, Oklahoma, Sheriff Marion VanHoesen examines a Panasonic two-speed microcassette recorder and body mike. The set cost the department roughly $250. (Photo by Ed Porter)

bad guys. Basically, I will look at listening and recording devices. Many of the things that hold true for one will also be true for the other, although there are some exceptions.

You have enough to worry about already when going undercover, so someone else (an electronics officer) should be in charge of the eavesdropping end of things, such as maintenance and troubleshooting. If the electronics officer does his job well, you will need to know little more than how to plant transmitters and recording devices, hide them beneath your clothes, and make sure you don't get caught doing either. But in the same vein as when my father used to warn me against investing in any business I couldn't step into and run myself, you need to know enough about the function of these devices to make sure the guy in charge is doing his job. Don't forget, your haunches will be on the line out there, not his.

Safety

Let's say you have arranged to buy an ounce of cocaine from a dealer named Red, and the buy is to go down in your motel room. The first decision to make is whether to use electronic devices at all. The safety of the undercover operative should always be the determining factor in this decision, since it goes without saying that losing a case because of lack of evidence is preferable to losing an officer. Ask yourself the following questions:

1) How likely is Red to check me for wires?
2) If he does check, and he finds electronic devices and concludes that I am a cop (or worse, an informant), how likely is he to get violent?
3) If he gets violent, how capable am I of handling things under the conditions specific to this situation?

The first two questions deal with Red's behavior, so the more information you can dig up about him before the buy, the better off you'll be. But no matter how well you think you know Red, you are trying to predict how another individual will react under a specific set of circumstances. You are really just guessing, and while you hope it will be an educated guess, it will be a guess nonetheless. There are criminals who will kill you and smile while they're doing it, and there are criminals who may become angry but, for psychological or physiological reasons, are not likely to do serious bodily harm. Ask yourself which of these categories Red falls into, then remember that you are still playing the odds, and you could be wrong with a capital W.

The third question deals with Red as part of the "conditions specific to this situation." Will he be alone? Will he be armed?—but it deals more with you. Cops can be divided into the same two categories as criminals: those capable of taking human life if necessary, and those who are incapable of doing so. You should have searched your soul long before this to determine where you stand, but when deciding whether to go on a case wired, you should do it again. Could you drop the hammer on Red if he finds the recorder and pulls a knife or gun on you? If you have any doubt, you should not meet this man wired. In fact, you should not go at all. Instead, consider whether you would be more comfortable filing reports than working undercover.

To Listen, Record, or Both?

Let's say that you've decided that using electronic devices is the correct path to take with Red. Next, you must decide exactly what you wish to accomplish with the bugs. Do you want a permanent record of the coke buy from Red? Do you want to enable your surveillance team to listen in on the transaction as it goes down? Do you want both? I'll look at recordings and transmissions separately and discuss why you would want one or both of them.

Recording

There are two reasons to record. The first, and most obvious, is so you'll have a play-by-play record of the transaction to present as courtroom evidence. But in the long run, the second reason may be even more valuable to you: a recording will enable you to critique every detail of your performance. You'll be able to hear the mistakes you made, review how well, or poorly, you explained those discrepancies, and note how your explanations were received. You will also probably deepen your faith in that god that watches over drunks and undercover officers when you discover other conspicuous blunders that the bad guys overlooked.

Case in point: I once reviewed an undercover videotape of an inexperienced (and ill-trained) officer in the process of purchasing a stolen car. I'll call him "Pete." The video opened with Pete and a car thief standing in a parking lot, waiting for another thief to deliver the vehicle. As they stood there, a black and white police car drove by on the street.

"What's that marked unit doing here?" Pete asked, nervously trying to sound like a real-life criminal afraid of being caught.

The car thief shrugged, and the matter was dropped as the marked unit drove out of the range of the lens. A few minutes later, the stolen car arrived, the deal went down, and other officers moved in to make the arrests.

Everything went smoothly for Pete on this deal, and he was very proud of his work until we pointed out a couple of very stupid mistakes that he made. First, a police car cruising quietly down a city street is hardly worthy of comment. True, anyone about to commit a felony will be watching for the cops, but these were experienced car thieves. (Pete would have known this had he done his homework.) Just like any other person with an IQ high enough to breathe, experienced criminals know that the police patrol the streets, and that means they drive down them. In a situation like this, the arresting officers would never show themselves until after the transaction is completed, and they would certainly not run surveillance in a marked unit.

The real sin, however, was Pete's use of the term "marked unit." To this day, thinking about it makes me shudder. When was the last time you heard a bad guy call a cop car a marked unit?

"Hey Mugsy, you seen any marked units around here?"

"No Bugsy, no marked units that I can see."

Marked unit is distinctive police "bureaucratese." Criminals do not use terms like this any more than they say "the party was contacted telephonically" when they make a phone call or "exercise caution" when they mean be careful. Call a marked unit a cop car, a police car, a pig wagon, or anything else you want to call it, but don't use gibberish that could only come out of the mouth of a cop.

These aren't the worst undercover mistakes ever made, but they are errors Pete might have made again had they not been brought to light via the recording. The next time he said marked unit, the bad guys might have been paying closer attention, and the entire operation could have been blown. And it could have been far worse for Pete *this* time, too. I happened to be acquainted with the two car thieves in the tape, and Pete's lucky that his wife isn't trying to get his life insurance company to pay off right now. The good news is, Pete never forgot his mistake. (That's because we never let him. The last I heard, his nickname was still Mark Unit, although most cops had shortened it to just Unit by then.)

Monitoring

There are two reasons for the members of your surveillance team to be able to hear the events of your transaction with Red as they unfold: 1) so they can testify in court as to what they heard and back up your testimony that Red indeed sold you an ounce of cocaine, and 2) so they will know, in a buy/bust situation, when it is time to move in and assist you in the arrest.

There is also a theory (Homesteaders who have never worked undercover endorse it widely) that since your surveillance team is listening, it will be able to ride in like the cavalry and save you if things go sour, but if you value your life, I wouldn't take this too seriously. A transmitter does ensure that your backup team will get there faster, but

The outside of this surveillance van looks no different from the one your next door neighbor drives. Inside, however, there are four marine batteries that operate a periscope, built-in tape recorder, heat and air conditioning unit, red and white interior lighting, and several electrical outlets. Other equipment includes a desk, refrigerator, storage compartment, and rifle/shotgun rack. (Photo by Ed Porter)

all this means is that rigor mortis will not have set into your joints by the time it gets there. Remember, you're always on your own when you work undercover.

Wearing vs. Planting Devices

Okay, you've decided that you want to use both recording and listening devices. Good decision. If Red finds a recorder, it won't make much of a difference if he finds a body mike, too. Now you must decide whether you will wear these instruments beneath your clothes or plant them in the area where the buy will go down.

Off-Body Plants

If it is feasible to hide the devices off-body, do so. Bad guys are less likely to pry the paneling off the walls of a motel room than they are to pat you down for wires. Even if the recorder or transmitter is found, you've got a better chance of talking your way out of the situation if you aren't wearing them. (Okay, not a great chance, but a chance just the same.) For example, if Red finds a microcassette recorder running under the motel room bed, he might be dumb enough to believe that it must have been left by the last occupant. But if he finds a Nagra reel-to-reel recorder in an elastic wrap around your chest and a microphone wire running down your sleeve, it will be pretty hard for you to convince him that you don't know how it all got there. Nobody is that dumb.

The problem with off-body plants is you rarely know for sure where the deal will go down. You've assumed that Red is coming to your motel room, but how do you know he won't knock on the door and insist that you come out to his car to get the coke? What if he tells you he didn't bring it, and you have to go with him to pick it up? That little Sony tape recorder you hid inside the TV isn't much good then, is it?

The decision as to where the bugs should be placed is yours, but here's what you're facing when you make it: it's much safer to plant the recorder off-body, but it's much more likely to be worthless because of unforeseen circumstances.

Wearing Devices on Your Person

Let's say you've decided to hide the recorder and transmitter on your person. Where it goes depends upon what clothes you're wearing and what specific equipment you will be using. Most of what holds true for the recording device will hold true for the transmitter as well, so I'll discuss wiring you with a recorder here and point out the differences when they come up.

If you are using a simple microcassette recorder, you may be able to just stick it in a pocket, with its internal microphone facing up. If the mike is sensitive enough, it may even pick up conversation if it is placed in your boot and covered with your pants leg, but do not count on it. You should thoroughly test this and any other carry method you intend to use beforehand. There are few things that are more depressing than taking the chance of getting caught wearing a recorder, and then finding out that you have no recording to compensate for the trouble you went through.

Whether you are using the cheapest bargain basement cassette recorder or one of the sophisticated devices put out by manufacturers like Nagra, you may find it necessary to use a remote microphone. Most microphones must be relatively unobstructed in order to pick up conversation, and since the recorder is harder to hide, its internal mike is usually buried beneath shirts, sweaters, or jackets.

If you are using a pocket carry, it will be necessary to cut holes in your clothing in order to run the connecting wire from the microphone to the recorder. Because of this, it is usually more practical to use an under-the-clothing carry. Here, you will want to use an elastic bandage or the pocketed chest strap that accompanies equipment designed specifically for surveillance.

Exactly where the recorder and transmitter are worn is very much like where you carry your weapon—it depends upon your clothing and specific body type. Under your arm or in the hollow at the small of your back are often good places, but you should experiment and find the right

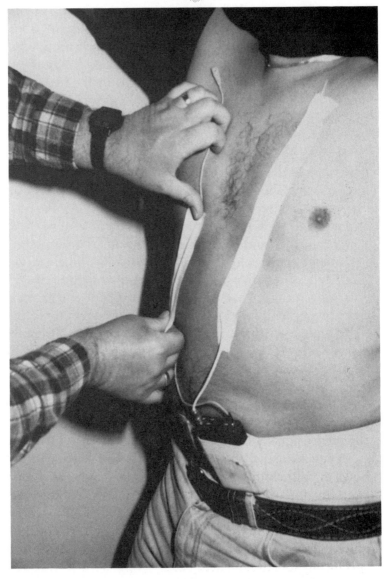

Remote microphones should be secured in a location where they will pick up as much conversation as possible. The belly-band supported transmitter, usually worn in the small of the back, has been moved to the front for photographic purposes. (Photo by Ed Porter)

place for you. Keep in mind that you must achieve both invisibility and security when you make this decision.

Microphone wires should be run from the recorder to a location at, or near, an opening in your clothing. Sleeves are usually the best place for this, although the collars of certain shirts and jackets sometimes work just as well. But keep in mind that each shirt, sweater, and jacket you own fits a little differently. To a certain degree, each time you "suit up" is unique unto itself, and, again, you must experiment with each outfit beforehand. Make sure that the mike will pick up conversation, regardless of what position you are in, and that the wire does not become exposed when you move.

Connecting wires have a nasty habit of disconnecting themselves with body movement. Make sure there is enough slack in the line to account for this, and secure all connections with tape. For the same reason, the power switch should be taped in the "on" position. I have found that duct tape works quite well in securing plugs and switches, and also takes up any slack in the elastic bandage or chest strap in which the recorder rides. (Unless you have distinct masochistic tendencies, I recommend shaving the areas of your body where the adhesive will make contact.)

When using transmitters, a stand-off distance of roughly 1/8 inch from the antenna is desirable to ensure optimum signal radiation, and there should always be at least one thickness of tape between the transmitter and your skin.

Backup Equipment

No matter how well electronic equipment is maintained or how frequently it is checked, there is always a chance that it will break, and that Homesteader Murphy decreed long ago that if it does, it will at the most inopportune time possible. For this reason, a backup recorder is a necessity, and a backup transmitter isn't a bad idea, either. This doubles the amount of equipment being used, and if you are able to plant the bugs off-body, this is no big deal. But if you think wearing one recorder and one transmitter is bad, wearing two of each is my idea of Hell on Earth. Not only is it uncomfortable and doubles your risk of exposure, you run out of room for guns and knives real fast.

When carrying backup transmitters, you don't have much choice; you just have to find another place to hide it. The transmitter works in league with your surveillance team's receiver, and if the microphone isn't positioned close enough to the action, it isn't going to function. Under controlled circumstances, you might choose to wear the primary transmitter and plant the backup, but you still run the risk of getting out of range of the backup if the main unit breaks down.

There is more flexibility in making a backup recording. Recordings can be made in one of two ways: 1) through a one-piece, self-contained unit on or about your person, or 2) by making the recording at the receiving end of the transmitter/receiver tandem. In other words, let the members of your surveillance team make the backup recording on their end. All they need to do is plug another tape recorder into their receiver and record while they listen.

VIDEO RECORDINGS

Video recordings are great, but you tempt fate even further than you do with audio recordings when getting them. Maybe by now the CIA or the Russians or Maxwell Smart have video recorders the size of your thumbnail, but those of us working within police budgets usually have to make do with the stuff from Radio Shack. Video recorders have become significantly smaller as technology has advanced, but I have yet to find one that I could strap under my shirt. Add to this the fact that the lens must be exposed and focused on the action, and your problems multiply. Under special circumstances, windowed briefcases can be used, but the window must be small (pinhole-lens cameras are now on the market), and if you take the briefcase into the motel room when you meet Red, make sure you have a story and a reason for it to be there, just like you do for yourself. You should also plan what you intend to do if Red wants to look inside it.

For the most part, any video recordings should be taken by the surveillance team, because they will more than likely require the use of special lenses and camouflage for the camera. Remember that each undercover operation is unique unto itself, and it will not be feasible to videotape every one. Video cameras are like all other electronic surveillance equipment; it is better not to use them than to use them at the risk of getting caught.

USING THE EQUIPMENT

As I stated earlier, you already have enough to worry about as an undercover operative, and another officer should be in charge of the electronic equipment. But there are certain functional aspects of these electronic devices that you must be familiar with, as you are responsible for their successful operation once the operation begins.

The basic components that make up a transmitter are the microphone, audio amplifier, power supply, modulator and oscillator, radio frequency amplifier, and antenna. If you're an electronics buff, you know all this already. If you're not, don't let it scare you. The only two things that can be controlled are the power supply and the antenna, anyway. The receiver antenna will be in the hands of the surveillance team, so that leaves you, the undercover officer, in control of the power supply.

If you are a secret agent for an organization like Greenpeace or the Sierra Club, you may use a transmitter powered by solar energy when you are on your quests to save whales and spotted owls. But if you operate in the real world with the rest of us, your power supply is going to come from batteries. Always check your batteries ahead of time with a multimeter, and if there is any doubt about their power, replace them. Use the multimeter to check new batteries as well—they may have been locked in the equipment locker (which is guarded by your Homesteader supervisor as if his wife's virtue were inside) since the turn of the century.

Most transmitters use what are known as "line of sight" frequencies. This means they travel in a straight line, which greatly restricts their working range. The higher the antennas are mounted, the greater the range. In theory, if both the transmitter and receiver antennas are mounted five feet off the ground, the working range will be approximately three miles (although other variables can enter into this). The surveillance team should mount the receiver antenna as high as possible in order to gain maximum range. You will be wearing the transmitter antenna, so your range will be more restricted. Assuming you are working at ground level, your antenna is going to be about five feet off the ground, unless you can jump like Michael Jordan.

Other electronic equipment that may be used when you work undercover are night vision scopes and goggles, time-lapse cameras, and other modern electronic wonders. But, like the function and maintenance of these devices, they fall outside the scope of this book. If you are interested in learning more, there is a wealth of material written on the subject.

Keep the use of electronics in undercover work in perspective. Be realistic as to what the instruments can and cannot do. Maintain your equipment, and never risk an undercover officer's life when it seems likely that the bad guys will check him for wires. Good luck, and may your 9-volt and AA batteries never run dry.

CHAPTER 11

The Care and Feeding of Informants

The basic steps for using informants are quite simple:

1) Interview your informant and reach a suitable agreement concerning what he will do for you, and what you, in turn, will do for him.
2) Establish the informant's credibility in the eyes of the court.
3) Use the informant to gather criminal intelligence and assist you in making felony cases.

Learning the steps is easy. Putting them into practice is considerably more complex.

DEALING WITH DIFFERENT TYPES OF INFORMANTS

How an informant is used depends upon what type or types of criminal cases he will be involved in, and which of the basic informant categories he falls into. To better explain this, I must return to the different informant types that were presented in Chapter 7.

The Con Working Off His Case

When attempting to roll over or "flip" a con you arrested, you'll more than likely conduct the initial interview at your office right after the bust. If he was busted by other officers and has not bonded out, you will probably have to use one of the visiting rooms at the county jail. If he's already bonded out and is on the streets, look him up. Regardless of where the interview takes place, make sure the two of you have complete privacy. You are going to ask him to turn informant, and he knows that unfortunate things can happen to informants when other bad guys find out what they're doing.

If your con has been down this road before, he'll know what you want before you ask. If he's new to the game, explain exactly what you're after and what you can and can't provide in return. You must not promise to have the charges against him dropped, or to get him a suspended sentence, or anything else that you can't back up. Simply tell him that if his work is satisfactory, you will give the prosecuting attorney your highest recommendation that he be cut some slack, and the prosecuting attorney will pass that recommendation on to the judge. You may tell him that you've done this many times before, and the judges have gone along with all of your suggestions to date. But make no guarantees, and make sure he knows from the start that the final decision is not in your hands. If you promise your con a suspended sentence and the judge refuses, word will get around on the streets, your current stable of informants will disappear, and your ability to procure new ones will evaporate.

If your con agrees to your terms, find out who he knows or, more importantly, who he can do. This is the only way to determine whether he's worth your time and effort. If he seems promising but is still in jail because he can't afford his bond, help him. Ask the district attorney's office to recommend a lower bond, or make arrangements through a

Recently arrested felons who face stiff stays in the penitentiary usually make the best informants. They have both the motivation and contacts to introduce you to other bad guys. (Photo by Edward Hasbrook)

cooperative bail bondsman, or do both. But do this as quietly as possible, and if you can't keep the arrest out of the newspapers, at least play it down as much as you can. The bad guys whom you want him to help you bust are familiar with this game, and they're always suspicious of felons who are out on bond.

Suppose your man agrees to work off his case as an informant and is back on the streets. So far, so good. His name is Ricky Brown, and he's a hard-core speed freak and mid-level dealer who made the mistake of selling you a thousand lot of white crosses. But Ricky doesn't want to testify in court against his supplier—a Jamaican named Rags—because he likes his testicles right where they are, not floating in a jar of formaldehyde on Rags' nightstand. That's okay, you don't want Ricky to testify anyway. Ricky is pretty much low-life human debris; to a jury he isn't going to look any better than Rags. The 12 men and women who are supposed to be Rags' peers really aren't. If they were, they would deal drugs and live in the same human sewer Rags haunts. They'd have felony convictions too, and if that were the case they'd have never made it onto the jury. No, the jurors who will eventually sit on Rags' case are from another walk of life, and they won't be able to make the distinction between an upright primate that sells 1,000 white crosses and one that sells 500,000. They'll say to themselves and each other, "Why should we believe Ricky? He sells drugs, too."

What you want from Ricky is for him to introduce you to Rags, so you have to establish Ricky as what the courts call a "reliable confidential informant." After he introduces you to Rags and you've formed your own relationship with the Jamaican, you cut Ricky out of the picture. But how do you do this? Since Ricky's first felony arrest probably occurred one minute after midnight on his 18th birthday, and his arrests have continued since then, you can't establish his reliability by showing that he is a good citizen. You will have to take another route.

Suppose Ricky has already told you that Sam Speed does a small white cross business out of his house at 1414 W. Amphetamine Avenue. Because word of Ricky's arrest may already be on the streets, drug dealers might be very hesitant to sell to him. As a rule, however, small dealers are less cautious than big dealers. It's like any other business—the less volume you do, the less picky you can be about your customers. This is one reason why Ricky's first buy should be small. Another reason to keep it small is simple economics. This is likely to be a "throwaway" buy. Your primary goal is not to make a case on Sam (although this may be an added benefit to the operation), it is to establish Ricky's reliability in order to convict Rags.

You meet with Ricky in a busy parking lot across the street from Sam's house and conduct a body search to make sure he is not "holding" (carrying illegal drugs on his person). (If he drives his vehicle to the buy site, it should be searched thoroughly as well.) You then provide Ricky with enough cash (with the serial numbers previously recorded) to make a small purchase. Stay in your car or somewhere else out of sight, and keep your eyes glued to Ricky until he enters Sam's house. As soon as Ricky comes back out of Sam's house, he should immediately hand the drugs and any remaining money over to you. You then conduct another body search to make sure he didn't score a little on the side for himself.

You can now swear that Ricky had no illegal substances in his possession when he entered the house, but he came out toting 100 little white pills with Xs on them. He also had less money in his possession than the amount you had given him, and, not surprisingly, the amount missing was equal to the current street price for a hundred lot of white crosses. If the transaction takes place within your sight—such as on the street—so much the better. You may be able to testify that you saw the drugs and the money change hands. But even if the transaction takes place inside the house, out of your sight, the situation is still controlled, because common sense dictates that Ricky purchased the amphetamines while he was in Sam's house. This should be enough to get a search warrant for Sam's house, but that's not what you're after.

What has transpired boils down to this: Ricky told you that Sam Speed sells dope at 1414 W. Amphetamine Avenue, and that he could go to that address and purchase the illegal substance, and then he did it. What Ricky told you proved to be true, and you are well on your way to establishing his reliability. To further establish Ricky's reliability in the eyes of the court, make a few more small buys—from other dealers if possible. You'll be killing two birds with one stone. Word will get around that Ricky is buying and no one is getting busted. This will reestablish his reliability in the eyes of the drug dealers, too.

When you are satisfied that you can swear to your informant's reliability in a court of law, have Ricky reestablish his connection with Rags. Then let him make a few buys from Rags on his own, with you following the same search procedures before and after each purchase, and document these cases. Your goal is to get Rags to trust Ricky again, and after Ricky makes a sufficient number of buys, and Rags doesn't go to jail, this should happen. But remember that Rags knows this game—he's a bigger dealer than Ricky, therefore he's probably smarter and more cautious. Selling to Ricky again is one thing; allowing Ricky to introduce him to a stranger who wants to buy is another.

Carefully evaluate everything Ricky tells you about the way Rags acts toward him. If Ricky is wired, record the conversations during the buys—not just for evidence, but so you can evaluate how much trust is reestablished between the two men. Do not have Ricky introduce you until you feel confident that Rags will be receptive. The time will never come when Rags says, "You know Ricky, I trust you so much, I'd even sell to a friend of yours whom I've never met." You will have to play things by ear and go with your instincts. Only when those instincts tell you the time is right will it be time for Rags to meet you.

The Good Citizen

Your initial interview with the good citizen informant is almost always the result of him approaching you rather than vice versa. The good citizen believes in doing his part to fight crime, and he finally gets the opportunity: Mr. Good discovers several potted marijuana plants being cultivated in one of his rental houses.

Mr. Good begins by making sure you know that he didn't want to rent the house to the two "hippies" in the first place, but his wife insisted they needed the money. He then asks in nervous roundabout ways if you think he might get killed for helping you. He has a TV set and goes to the movies too, you see.

You do not need to discuss terms with Mr. Good—all he wants out of this is the knowledge that he has done the right thing and a little excitement in his otherwise humdrum life. If he is truly a good citizen, his criminal record will be no more serious than a few speeding tickets. Therefore, his credibility in the eyes of the court can be established easily.

But there's a problem: he's honest and reliable, but what can he really do to help? Give you a key to the rental house and permission to go in? Sure, he can do that, but check your state statutes first regarding the rights of each party entering into a renter/rentee relationship. These laws vary from jurisdiction to jurisdiction. If Mr. Good saw the marijuana plants upon entering the house after the tenants requested that he fix the plumbing, he had a legal right to be inside. If he simply went in to snoop around, you are on thinner ice. But if you can establish that Mr. Good had a right to be inside the house when he saw the plants and determine that he knows marijuana from ragweed, poison ivy, and magnolias, you are in pretty good shape.

This is, however, a specialized case. More often you will encounter the good citizen who tells you that the guy who lives down the block from him is selling drugs. I'll call him Mr. Two Shoes. When you ask Mr. Two Shoes how he knows, he'll say, "Because cars come at all hours of the day and night, and they never stay more than 15 minutes." Then, with a knowing smirk, he'll add, "What does that tell you?"

Well, it tells you exactly what it tells him—the guy down the street is selling dope. The problem is, it doesn't tell that to a court of law. You need much more than suspicion to obtain a search warrant, and what can Mr. Two Shoes do to help you get it? Go to the guy's house to borrow a cup of sugar? Or are you going to send him in to make a buy like you did with Ricky? Mr. Two Shoes is the president of the Rotary Club, a deacon in the First Baptist Church, and a Little League baseball coach. If the guy down the street is really selling dope, Mr. Two Shoes is going to get the door slammed in his face.

While his heart is in the right place, there's often not much he can do to help because he's known to be a good citizen. The bad guys don't trust him much more than they do you. So listen to him, smile and nod, and explain why

This good citizen has the motivation—she wants to do the right thing—but unless unique circumstances enter the picture, she will not possess the criminal connections to do much good. (Photo by Edward Hasbrook)

it's not going to work out. At the same time, remain open to the possibility that the long shot may come through. There might be an isolated incident where he can be of use, such as in the example of Mr. Good and the rental house.

The Revenger

The informant whose motive is revenge usually comes to you just like a good citizen does. He might even be a crossover informant: a good citizen who has a bone to pick with somebody. In any case, as stated earlier, he can come from any walk of life. Johnny, the revenger informant I discussed in Chapter 7, had no criminal record and was just flat pissed off that someone was trying to seduce his wife. Can't say I blame him. He may never have been elected mayor or worked as a fund-raiser for the United Way, but because he had a clean record, his credibility could be established as easily as a good citizen's.

If you get a potential revenger whose track record looks like Rodney King's, however, you'd have to establish his reliability the same way you would with the con working off his case. Regardless of which route you take, the revenger's job is the same as any other informant's—to gather intelligence and assist you in making criminal cases.

While revengers often have no felony conviction record, more often than not they are at least acquainted with people from the seedier side of society. If so, they can operate within certain boundaries. If not, unless they have some special situation like Mr. Good and his rental house, they will be about as useless as the good citizen. Watch them closely. Like mercenary informants, they are sometimes tempted to set up their enemy in order to speed up the "justice" process.

The Mercenary

You may be able to establish the merc's credibility using his past performance working for other departments, bureaus, or agencies. If not, establish his credibility as you

The informant motivated by revenge is often helpful but must be watched closely to make sure he doesn't "manufacture" evidence. (Photo by Edward Hasbrook)

would the con's, or, if possible, as you would when dealing with the good citizen by proving that he is a good, reliable member of the community. This method is not likely to work very well, however, because if the merc is able to move within the criminal community with the freedom it takes to be a competent informant, it is highly unlikely that he is without sin himself.

One of the strongest mercs I ever worked with was a woman I'll call "Gwen." Gwen had the uncanny ability to operate at all levels of society. She was as comfortable drinking Manhattans and flirting with U.S. Senators at a campaign fund-raiser as she was wearing ragged blue jeans and scoring crank from a Hell's Angel. One night, I sent Gwen into a college fraternity party to buy Ecstasy. Two hours later, she changed into her motorcycle jacket and bought acid at a hard-core lesbian bar. The woman was flexible.

Gwen's motive was simple: money. She'd do anything and everything (if you get my drift) to endear herself to her prey, and she had the body, looks, and charm to pull it off. You didn't have to worry about Gwen setting anyone up—she didn't need to. She was just too good. What you did have to worry about was falling in love with her, muddying up your cases for court and making a damn fool of yourself in the process. Not every undercover officer I know who fell in love with Gwen pulled this off. Sometimes good cases had to be sacrificed, and more than one undercover officer's marriage bit the dust in Gwen's wake. I'll talk more about situations like this in the chapter on personal traps. And no, I never did.

INFORMANT OR SNITCH?

I have discussed the importance of good informants in every chapter so far, and if you are a cop, you've probably noticed that not once have I referred to them by a term we all use: snitches. There is a very good reason for this. This word, and other derogatory terms used for the men and women who help you make cases, should evaporate from your vocabulary as of now.

Like all slang terms, the contemptuous nomenclature for informants varies from region to region and from time period to time period. Snitches, squealers, singers, stool pigeons—call them what you will when they aren't within earshot, but never call a snitch a snitch to his face. The word conjures up grammar school memories of tattletales—an image nobody wants. (Do you remember what you and your friends used to do to tattletales after school? That's right, you used to beat them up.)

A snitch is exactly what your informant is. He already knows it, and he doesn't need to be reminded. Call him a snitch, and watch his face drop and his work fall off. Call him an operative, or agent, or even a spy, and watch his face light up and his efforts to help you double.

THE PSYCHOLOGY OF INFORMANTS

The vast majority of informants are like Ricky Brown; they're not much better human beings than Rags or the other bad guys they go after. The con working off his case may be even worse, but the offense you hold over his head is less serious than the crimes of the bad guys he can help you arrest. With the exception of the good citizens, informants have less-than-admirable reasons for doing what they do: they want to stay out of prison, they're doing someone in for the money, or they just flat hate somebody and want to see bad things happen to him.

Informants Have Feelings, Too

No, I am not suggesting that you give your informants hugs, start a support group for them, or do any of the other ridiculous "touchy feely" things of the late 20th century. I am simply reminding you that even if your informants are of dastardly character, they are human beings—at least most exhibit the same emotions as human beings. One of these feelings is shame, and whether they express their shame to you or not, they generally feel at least a certain amount of it for what they do.

I can almost hear you now. You say you don't give a damn how that snitch of yours feels? You say he deserves all the shame and guilt that can find its way into his godforsaken semi-sociopathic soul? Well, I can't argue with you— you're right. But remember that your prime objective is not to punish your informants for their crimes—you are trying to get them to help you open the penitentiary door for even "badder" bad guys.

Browbeating your informants is almost always counterproductive. Think about it. Do you work better when you believe in your objective 100 percent, or when you're questioning the validity of your task? Do you work better when you feel good about yourself, or when you wonder if you're any better than the dirtbags you arrest? (All

Explorers have moments like this—the Homesteaders make sure of it.)

Informants are no different from you in this respect. If you want them to do a good job, you must periodically reinforce the fact that they are doing the right thing. The old saying, "there's a little bit of good in the worst of us" applies here, and you can use it to your advantage. Except for full-blown sociopaths, most criminals rationalize their aberrant behavior the same way you excuse your own transgressions. You tell yourself things like, "Okay, I drink too much and gamble a little, but at least I don't cheat on my wife." Your informant tells himself, "Okay, I sold marijuana, but I'm helping bust heroin dealers." However, there are exceptions to this rule.

Establishing Who's in Charge

Once in a while, you may find yourself working with an informant who needs to be brought down a notch or two. Instead of referring to him as a snitch, you took my advice and called him your operative or secret agent. The problem is, he took you seriously. Since then, you have watched him evolve from a beaten and subservient person to someone who thinks he's James Bond saving the Queen. He's convinced that he's so valuable, he should be telling *you* what to do.

Do not allow this to happen. You are in charge, and you must remain so. This does not mean that you should not listen to your informant's suggestions, but they should remain just that—suggestions, not orders. If you find that your informant has developed such "delusions of grandeur," you may have to remind him that you reserve the right to terminate the relationship and return him to jail.

Try the polite approach first. Something like, "Have you forgotten who is in charge here, Denny?" If that doesn't work, increase the threat slightly. "Would you rather go back to prison?" If the knowledge of who is running the show still doesn't return to his mind, something a little less

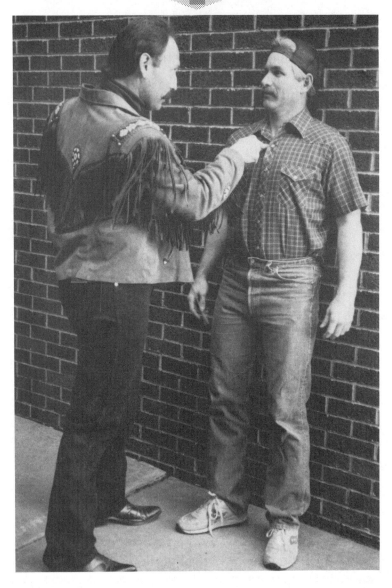

Informants, particularly the cons and mercenaries, must be reminded occasionally of who is in charge of the investigation. (Photo by Edward Hasbrook)

subtle may be called for: "Shut your fuckin' mouth and do your fuckin' job, or you'll be bending over for the big boys in the penitentiary" may be just the ticket that returns him to reality. Punctuate this with a brotherly punch in the arm or something of that nature, and this can be very effective in reestablishing the proper fraternal bond necessary to the relationship. Who says I'm not a sensitive modern man?

Motivation

Motivating your informant to do good work is essential, and in doing so you must remember that each one has a unique personality and will respond differently to each stimulus. (A PhD in psychology would be handy here, but if you had that, you'd have a job that made real money, wouldn't you?) Be aware of your informant's priorities, beliefs, and needs. This is the only way to know which "carrots" to dangle in front of his nose. There are times to be sympathetic, compassionate, and responsive, and there are other times to kick ass. Some informants must be relaxed to work well. Others won't get off their butts and do their job until you've scared them within an inch of their lives.

I have no intention of taking credit for the following example, nor is any undercover team I ever knew responsible. I heard about it, and no one seems to know who the guys were who actually did it. That's my story, and I'm sticking to it.

Once upon a time there were two undercover partners I'll call "Smith" and "Jones." Smith and Jones knew that some informants only worked well if their "keepers" scared them even more than the bad guys. So the two officers developed a unique and very effective method of achieving this state of mind in their charges.

When an informant's attention wandered from his priorities and needed to be brought back on track, Smith and Jones would pick him up in their undercover car and drive him into the country, out of view of prying eyes. Both officers would yell and scream the whole way, threatening everything from decapitation to castration if the informant did not start making cases. Upon reaching an isolated grove of trees, Smith would pull the car off the road and produce a sawed-off 16-gauge single-shot shotgun. Both men's screams and threats would reach a crescendo as Smith shoved the weapon into the informant's mouth.

This pandemonium would continue until one of the officers finally said, "Fuck it! Let's just kill him and get it over with."

At this point, Smith would pull the trigger. The hammer would fall on an empty chamber, of course, but their objective was achieved. They had the informant's undivided attention, and he almost always returned to work and made the cases he'd promised to make.

Am I suggesting that you violate the civil rights of the scum you deal with in order to stimulate their enthusiasm? Of course not. I'm simply relating a story I heard.

But wait—there's more.

One day, Smith picked up Jones and they drove to the apartment house where one of their informants lived. Jones waited in the car while Smith went up to get the man. While he waited, Jones pulled the sawed-off 16-gauge shotgun out from under the seat and broke it open. He was surprised to see that the chamber was empty, since unless they were planning to engage in their little melodrama, they always kept it loaded as an extra precaution. The informant they were using that night had proven to be one of the most dependable and trustworthy ones they'd ever had. Therefore, it never occurred to Jones that Smith might be intending to use the shotgun as a throat swab.

Jones reached in the glove compartment, opened a box of 16-gauge shells, loaded the weapon, and returned it to the floorboard, all the while planning to reprimand his partner and remind him that the two most useless things in the world are a dull knife and an empty gun.

Smith returned with the informant, and they drove to a service station and filled the gas tank. This time, the informant and Smith waited while Jones went into the station and paid for the gas. He returned, and Smith began driving out of town.

Jones had other things on his mind, so he didn't catch on to what was happening, and Smith didn't even start yelling until they'd reached the grove of trees. Then it suddenly dawned on Jones that Smith had unloaded the shotgun on purpose. More importantly, Jones realized that he had reloaded the weapon in his partner's absence, and Smith thought the 16-gauge's chamber was still empty.

By this time the shotgun barrel was in the informant's mouth, and Smith was howling so loud he couldn't hear Jones' screams. Jones' last thought before Smith pulled the trigger was where they were going to bury the body so the coyotes wouldn't dig it up.

Smith pulled the trigger, and just like always, the hammer fell on the empty chamber with a loud metallic clink. Smith and the informant began laughing hysterically. Between tears, Smith explained that he had indeed forgotten to reload the sawed-off shotgun after its last performance and remembered while Jones was paying for the gas. When he discovered that Jones had already reloaded it, he and the informant quickly cooked up the practical joke. It had worked better than they expected it to, and everyone lived happily ever after. Except for Jones, who had to be driven home for a clean pair of underwear.

*Special footnote to all American Civil Liberties Union attorneys: Let me stress that I don't know these two guys. Mark was not Smith. I was not Jones. These outrageous incidents did not occur in a 1977 Ford Grenada with Kansas plates, and the sawed-off 16-gauge shotgun was not a gift from a sheriff for whom we had worked.

CHAPTER 12

Creating Illusions

There will be times when even the combination of an informant's introduction and your Oscar-award-winning undercover performance will not be enough to make your target trust you. In other words, if he is a burglar, he will suspect that instead of being the fellow burglar you claim to be, you are a cop. If he is a drug dealer, he will suspect that instead of being a user or another dealer, you are a cop. If he is an armed robber looking for a getaway driver, he will suspect that you are lying about all those times you won the Indianapolis 500. And why would you be lying? Right, because you are a cop. So you have to convince him that you're not a cop.

If you have enough time to invest, time may be all it takes to accomplish this. On the other hand, it might not be, and few of us are allocated that much time anyway. There are two alternatives: 1) forget it, or 2) take more elaborate steps to solidify your undercover identity and convince him that you are, indeed, a bad guy just like him.

How is this accomplished? Look at what bad guys do for a moment. Drug dealers deal dope, thieves steal, robbers rob, and murderers murder. So what do you need to do to convince the criminal you want to bust that you aren't a cop? Simply deal dope, steal, rob, and murder before his very eyes. You say you see a problem here? Okay, you don't really rob, kill, deal, and steal. You just create the illusion that you're doing these things. (Warning for Homesteaders: The information contained in this chapter has been known to produce strokes, heart attacks, and bleeding ulcers in members of your species.)

SAFETY AND LEGAL CONCERNS

Before reading the following, consider this very carefully: if you choose to recreate the following illusion or create similar ones of your own, you will be walking a very thin line between doing your job as a police officer and breaking the law. More importantly, every step of the way you will find traps that must be avoided or you, or someone else, will get hurt. Performed correctly and with control over the situation, these illusions can be and have been created both successfully and legally, but you will be taking certain calculated risks. At any time, any of a thousand outside influences can suddenly jump up to "bite you on the ass." The slightest oversight on your part can produce grievous results. If the defendant's case goes to court, the illusions you created will be brought up by the defense, and it will attempt to make it look as though you are guilty of felonies yourself. Therefore, you must carefully document each step of your illusion so you can refute such accusations.

If you decide to create an elaborate illusion, you must engage in equally elaborate planning. Regardless of how small or insignificant it may seem, each detail must be gone over meticulously. You and everyone else involved in your illusion must not enter into it lightly. You'll probably have a lot of fun, but don't ever start thinking it's a game.

All right, let's lighten up a little now. The last couple of paragraphs were a serious warning, but they were also designed to weed out any Homesteaders who might have slipped though the first 11 chapters. If you're still with me, you must be an Explorer, so let's get rolling and have some fun.

THE ANATOMY OF CREATING AN ILLUSION

Okay boys and girls, in this illustration there's a house burglar who's about to carry away the entire south end of Detroit, or Los Angeles, or Waukomis, Oklahoma, or whatever other city you'd like it to be. These burglaries have been going on for almost a year, and a suit-and-tie detective sergeant tells you it's Jimmy Gloves who's pulling them off. How does he know? The burglaries started a week after Jimmy made parole, they take place between 0100 and 0400 hours on Sundays, and fingerprints are never found—all earmarks of Jimmy's work. But just as important, Detective Sergeant Suit-and-Tie just knows in his gut that it's Jimmy. This is enough evidence for you and me and the sergeant, but it won't get you a conviction. In fact, it won't even get the case to court.

Enter the Informant

But voila! As you and Detective Sergeant Suit-and-Tie are sitting drinking the bad coffee they make upstairs in the burglary division, you remember that you busted Sammy Cohort two nights ago on possession of stolen property, and you've already rolled him over to your side. Best of all, Sammy mentioned Jimmy Gloves during his soul-cleansing interview. Sammy and Jimmy are tight—at least that's what Sammy said.

The next thing you know, you and your new informant are on your way to the local bar where Jimmy Gloves hangs out when he's not stealing. Sammy is going to introduce you as both a fellow thief and a fence. (In this economy, who can live on one job anymore?) He's not going to use the words "thief" or "fence" when he introduces you. Instead, he'll let Jimmy know in the roundabout way those things get done. Also, Sammy won't make it clear what you steal or how you go about stealing it—you'll see why in a little bit.

The introduction is made and Jimmy is cordial. But after three games of eight ball and twice as many beers, you are reminded of something: informants have a tendency to stretch the truth.

Sammy said that he and Jimmy were tight. Well, it's clear that they know each other—but they aren't the intimate chums Sammy claimed they were. By the time you and Sammy say good night, it is obvious that Jimmy Gloves would cannibalize his own mother before he'd take you along on a burglary or sell you anything he's stolen.

You can go back to the bar the next night, and the next, and the next. You can shoot pool with Jimmy for a few years and hope that one day he'll decide that you and he are of the same breed and that he can trust you. Or, you can speed up the process by creating an illusion.

Gaining the Bad Guy's Trust

Take an overall look at the situation. Jimmy has not approached you either as a fence or burgling colleague. That's no big deal; no thief in his right mind who'd just met you would. Regardless of how much Jimmy needs help on his next job or wants a new place to get rid of stolen goods, he's cautious. Since it's much too soon for you to approach him and ask for a piece of his action, why not invite Jimmy into a deal of your own?

Jimmy is a house burglar, so you must make your "job" something else. You don't want to infringe on his territory, and, equally important, you don't want to enter his specialty where he might think he's in charge. You must run the show. You want Jimmy to feel a little hesitant, a little uncomfortable; like he's just a wee bit out of his ballpark.

At the same time, you've got to make sure that it's not so far removed from what he knows that he won't be interested. If you can reach a happy medium, he'll be taken off guard just enough so that he'll willingly follow your direction. This reduces the odds that he will do anything unexpected. I said reduce—not eliminate. You will still have to keep your eye on him every step of the way during the robbery.

Oh, did I forget to tell you? You're about to commit an armed robbery.

Don't push things. Get to know Jimmy, and while you're letting him beat you at eight ball, drop a few hints that you and Sammy might be the ones behind the recent convenience store heists. Then, when you feel the time is right, have Sammy make your move since he knows Jimmy better. Sammy's story is that the two of you have cased the convenience store on the corner of Boulevard and Main. You've learned that it does good business right up until it closes at midnight, and that whoever is working the last shift periodically takes the money out of the cash register and drops it through the slot in the floor safe. One night you saw the girl on duty open the safe when she needed more change, which means the crap they put out about the cashier not knowing the combination is just that—crap.

You already have a plan, but it requires a third man. You will enter the store one minute before closing time and conduct the robbery while Sammy, who has already ripped off one of the store's uniform shirts, turns the sign around and stands at the door, smiling and telling any customers making a last-minute dash for Ding-Dongs that he is sorry, the store is closed. But these activities keep both of you occupied and away from the car, which means you need a driver.

"Jimmy, are you interested?"

Jimmy should hesitate. He's a burglar, not an armed robber. But, as I said, you want him to feel a little uncomfortable. You're hoping that he will just sit there with the motor running and try not to urinate in his pants while he waits on the 25 percent of the take that you offered him. But what if he's so hesitant that he refuses? Sweeten the pot a little. Stress how much business you see the store doing, and how much easy money he'll make for doing nothing but driving. Offer him up to 30 percent of the take if you have to, but cut it off somewhere around there. You and Sammy are doing the real work, and if you agree to give Jimmy too much of the take, he'll know something is amiss.

If he still refuses, then forget it. Find another way into his heart, or move on to another bad guy and leave Jimmy for the next time around.

Carrying Out the Crime

Let's say Jimmy agrees to help you. You plan for the robbery to go down on Friday night, when you claim the store does even more business than on Saturday. (Remember Jimmy burgles houses on Sunday mornings, so don't give him an excuse not to be involved by planning it for that day.)

Are you wondering how you are going to get out of doing the robbery? The answer is simple: you aren't. You are going to rob the store.

Unbeknownst to Jimmy, the convenience store is owned by Frank Family, the brother-in-law of Detective Sergeant Suit-and-Tie. Frank has agreed to go along with the ruse, and he's even volunteered to work the designated Friday night shift himself. Frank isn't a very brave man, and he's a little scared he could get hurt. But he's even more scared that Suit-and-Tie will tell his sister that his new employee, that cute little blond with the Dolly Parton breasts, has a much broader job description than she thinks.

At 11:59 Friday night, Jimmy pulls the car up in front of the convenience store. (Make sure he parks where he can see the action through a window.) You and Sammy go in, start looking at Hostess Twinkies, and wait for the last customer, a guy wearing a plaid sport coat, to leave. Behind the counter, Frank keeps giving you the eye nervously, and you hope that if Jimmy notices this, he'll chalk it up to the fact that you and Sammy look suspicious and that it's closing time, which is always the ideal time for a robbery.

The customer leaves, and Sammy pulls off his jacket, which was covering his convenience store uniform shirt, and walks to the door. You hurry to the counter and draw your gun. As Frank opens the safe, his expression indicates that his pants are the ones that will be wet when all of this is over, not Jimmy's. Out of the corner of your eye, you see Sammy crack open the glass front door and hear him say, "Sorry ma'am, we're closed." You breathe a silent sigh of relief when the old woman with the umbrella walks away without arguing.

A moment later, Frank hands you a paper sack filled with small bills, and you order him to lie down on the floor behind the counter. Then, before you realize that you've pulled it off, you and Sammy are back in the car with Jimmy, speeding away and cackling like maniacs about how easily the whole thing went down. What you are experiencing is called "robber's high," and it is often as much the motive behind armed robberies as the money.

The adrenaline rush has waned a little by the time you reach your informant's house to divide the spoils of your labor. You are a little disappointed that there was less money than you'd anticipated, but hey, it was free. You and Jimmy leave Sammy's house, and just before you drop Jimmy off at the bar, you see that he has a new respect for you in his eyes. Yes, Jimmy Gloves, the eight-ball-playing house burglar, respects you. More importantly, he trusts you. You're going to be the first person to pop into his mind the next time he needs someone to go on a job with him.

The illusion you have created is complete, and you go home thinking, "Man, was that easy or was that easy?" You're right; in this imaginary example, things couldn't have gone better. But imaginary is the operative word, and unexpected complications almost always arise when you attempt something like this.

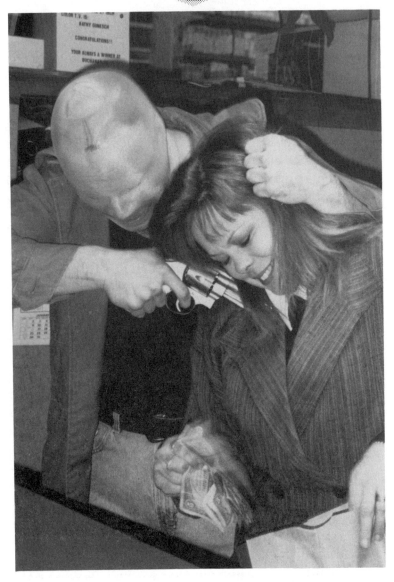

Faking a robbery is extremely complex and dangerous. Careful planning and control of all aspects of the illusion are essential. (Photo by Edward Hasbrook)

Careful Planning and Creativity

Let's look at a few of the operational problems that you had to overcome before this illusion took place. Although the illusion you decide to create will not be identical to this one, the operational obstacles you encounter may be similar in some respects. Just remember to be creative.

Finding "Franks"

Where do you find a "Frank"? In Chapter 3, I pointed out the fact that a surprising number of citizens are willing to lend you their automobile to be used undercover, but lending you their store is an entirely different matter. In many cases, they will not only be taking a financial risk, but a personal risk as well. Make sure they fully understand this, and find out exactly where you stand both criminally and civilly. While the worst possible scenario need not be the deciding factor when determining whether to proceed with or terminate an operation that requires the use of someone's property, being aware of it will at least give you the opportunity to approach the operation with your eyes open.

Frank was willing to cooperate because Detective Sergeant Suit-and-Tie held a hammer over his head that was not unlike the ones we often wield to influence informants to cooperate. Keep in mind, though, that you are not dealing with some dirt-bag felon here, but an honest American citizen. If he understands the risk and agrees to go through with it, he deserves a pat on the back from you, and maybe a letter from the mayor when all is done. But you have no moral right to coerce any law-abiding citizen into grave risk of bodily harm. We could talk about criminal charges and civil liability, but the bottom line is "it just ain't right."

Keep your eyes and ears open for Franks as you go about your daily routine, and when you find one, file him in the back of your mind for future reference. You may find a cooperative citizen in the ex-cop who left the department and did well with his fast-food franchise. He's glad he's making more money, but he might miss police work.

Sheriff's departments usually have part-time "posses" and other agencies sponsor reserve or auxiliary forces. These are often comprised of people who are in a good position to help you through their full-time occupation.

Don't forget old friends. The guys you played high school football with or the girl who broke your heart in college may be of assistance. Good citizens who are willing to pitch in above and beyond the call of duty are out there—you just have to look for them.

Reimbursing Frank's Money

You're going to steal Frank's money, so who covers the loss? It'll either be Frank, your agency, or you. The robbery wasn't real, so Frank can't file an insurance claim—that's known as insurance fraud, and you should make sure he knows that ahead of time. In this case, you can return both yours and Sammy's cut, meaning a net loss of only Jimmy's 25 percent. Frank might be willing to cover that as part of his contribution to a better world. If not, see if you can swing it through your supervisors. The last resort is you. I know you don't make enough money to be able to afford to do this, but Frank can "lighten" his safe ahead of time. (Remember how disappointed you, Sammy, and Jimmy were when there wasn't as much money as you'd expected?) Decide how light you can make the take without Jimmy getting suspicious, then determine if it is worth the 25 percent of it that will come out of your pocket to make the case.

Getting Permission

The next and perhaps even harder task, depending upon your particular position, is getting the "bureaucratic okay." As soon as you present your idea, expect a Homesteader to immediately look for reasons why you can't do it. Make sure you have all the political bases covered before you breathe a word of what you are considering to anyone, and be prepared to defend your plan in a pleasant and nonthreatening manner. This will not be fun, but it can be a positive experience. Use the Homesteader as a devil's advocate—he can open your eyes to some of the potential problems you missed—but be ready to think on your feet just as fast as you would if a dope dealer had a gun to your head. Don't just tell the Homesteaders that you're sure it will work; show them how it will work and convince them that no one will get hurt.

Expect the Unexpected

There are a few things that could have gone wrong with this illusion. First, when your gun's barrel was jammed into Frank's left nostril, your old friend Murphy could have decided it was time to play a number of little tricks on you. For instance, any patrolman in that section of town might have been passing by the store when he remembered he was out of Marlboros. Unless the patrol shift had been alerted to what you had planned to do, you would have been lying on the convenience store's floor tile with a .40 S&W Black Talon in the side of your head.

What if you didn't notice a customer who was bent over behind the magazine rack at the rear of the store? That's right, the one who didn't straighten up until you screamed, "This is a robbery!" What are you going to do if he turns out to be a legally armed citizen who wants to become a hero? What if he's an off-duty cop? Even though every uniformed officer working the division has been ordered to stay away from the store that night, this guy may work on the other side of town. His shift wasn't alerted, and he just happened to stop in the store for something on his way home. Of course, I could be wrong. Instead of working on the other side of town, the guy who will be aiming the little off-duty Firestar .45 at you might not even be with your department. He might be a deputy sheriff, or a federal agent, or from one of the city's suburb forces. Whoever he is, he stopped in to pick up a quart of milk on his way home, stumbled onto this robbery in progress, and now he's going to kill you.

Have you notified every cop who lives or works within a hundred miles of the store? Have you sent out memos to every citizen with a concealed carry license? If so, you've still missed everyone carrying a gun without a license. Not that it matters at this point, because Jimmy decided not to come along. If every cop and legally armed citizen knew what you were doing, Jimmy would have heard about your little ploy long ago.

Letting all these officers and citizens in on your illusion would have been asinine. But to illustrate how impossible it is to eliminate all risk, let's assume that you did, and, miraculously, Jimmy didn't hear about it and is waiting in the car outside. A lieutenant from the Home Town, Arkansas, Police Department is in town on vacation and is staying at the motel next to the store. He knows as well as you do that you can be in the wrong place at the wrong time, and he's made the same decision you probably make when you're out of your jurisdiction and can't legally carry a weapon: it makes more sense to break a minor law than to end up in a body bag.

You can't possibly keep everyone out of the store who might be carrying a gun, and if you do your job well, the armed robbery will appear as real to them as it does to Jimmy. I'm not saying don't go through with your illusion; the odds are low that something like this will happen. But the odds are there, nonetheless, and you must never forget that long shots sometimes come through, even though they didn't come through at Frank's convenience store that night.

Moving on to other potential disasters, what would you have done if the cute little blond employee who got Frank into this to begin with had come screaming out of the supply room? Sure, Frank promised you that no other employees would be in the store, but he couldn't resist bragging to "Dolly" about how he was doing his part to fight crime. Dolly wanted to watch, and since Frank figured you'd never know, he hid her in the supply room. But Dolly's a flake—she panicked, and now she's running out the front door screaming.

Jimmy sees her, but there's nothing to worry about, right? You told Jimmy before the job that all guns were to be ditched. The only piece you wanted along was the one you'd be carrying. Did Jimmy follow your order? I don't know, and neither do you. But what are those loud bangs you just heard in front of the store?

Don't forget the old lady with the umbrella who was nice enough to move on when Sammy told her the store was closed. What if she hadn't been so cooperative? What if she had stood there and argued, or looked through those coke-bottle trifocals, saw what was happening at the counter, and dropped dead from a heart attack on the sidewalk?

Last, but not least, remember the customer who was at the checkout counter when you arrived? That's right, the guy in the plaid sport coat. The customer behind the magazine rack might not have been an off-duty cop, but this one was. A smart cop, too—the smell of a robbery about to go down was as thick in his nostrils as a two-week-old corpse in mid-July. So he backed his car out of the parking lot and circled the block to the alley at the rear of the store. He keeps a 12-gauge Ithaca pump in the trunk of his car, and he is hiding around the corner where Jimmy can't see him. He and eight rounds of double-aught buckshot are waiting for you and Sammy when you come out the front door.

What else might have happened that you hadn't counted on? A thousand variations of each of these unexpected intrusions, and a thousand more other potential problems that I could describe if I had the space. Add to this a thousand things I haven't thought of that you won't think of either, and you'll probably cover about 10 percent of what could conceivably go wrong.

It is vitally important to be in control of the situation in every aspect of undercover work, and it is even more important if you choose to create an illusion such as the one above. You must plan for and eliminate all problems that you can think of ahead of time. Then you must realize that you have overlooked more than you foresaw and be ready to make split-second decisions, and pray a lot.

A CLOSING ARGUMENT

All through this chapter, I heard a voice out there screaming, "Entrapment! Entrapment! You talked Jimmy into going along! You can't file the case!" Whoever is saying this must be a Homesteader. As you Explorers already know, this is not entrapment because we never intended to file armed robbery charges on Jimmy. No actual crime was committed. Jimmy just *thinks* you robbed a store. He knows that police officers are not allowed to rob, so it follows that you cannot be a cop. Not only are you not a cop, you are a bad guy just like him. Furthermore, Jimmy thinks he has something on you and can hold the robbery over your head if he needs to. After all, he was only the driver and could undoubtedly cut a deal to testify against you. We all believe in illusions of one type or another, and Jimmy is living under the one created here. So wait for him to call and ask you to go on a burglary with him or fence some stolen property.

With a little inventiveness and a lot of careful planning, the illusions you are capable of creating are limitless. You can appear to be a burglar, drug dealer, or even a murderer. So get to work, and use the creativity and imagination that God gave you and left the Homesteaders without. It's part of what makes undercover work more fun than directing traffic.

CHAPTER 13

Developing Memory

One of the first things you learned at the academy was that a good cop always carries a pen and notebook. The reason is obvious: your memory plays tricks on you and becomes distorted over time or just plain disappears altogether. A few well chosen notes can prevent this from happening. They refresh your recollections for court testimony and can sometimes be introduced as evidence themselves. I hope you learned this, and I hope you put it into practice when you were in uniform or wearing a suit and tie. It's good advice. Now forget it.

Criminals associate the carrying of writing instruments with cops. They have seen the traffic cop pull out his pen and citation book after he's stopped them for speeding, and they've watched detectives take notes while interrogating them for more serious crimes. They know that real estate agents, bookies, doctors, and just about everyone else in the world takes notes of one kind or another, but they also know that not many people keep a notebook and pen on their person at all times. Except cops.

Having a Papermate pen sticking out of your shirt or the spiral wire of a small notebook eating its way through the frayed hip pocket of your Levi's may not be as bad as pinning your badge to your T-shirt, but it's not that far off. It will draw a criminal's attention your way, and he will begin to wonder why you feel it necessary to jot things down, what your notes involve, and whether or not his name appears in them. Even if you've had a great introduction by an informant, played your undercover role flawlessly, and perhaps even created a more elaborate illusion under which your target is operating, you are still the new kid on the block. The bad guys will retain at least a mild curiosity about you for a long, long time, and you don't want to add any fuel to the fires of their imaginations.

You have already seen many examples of how the rules of good police work change drastically when you put on

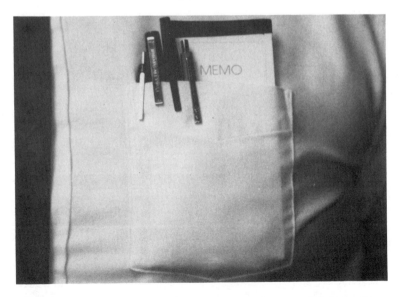

This is a good example of how NOT to appear undercover. (Photo by Gary Campbell)

your beard. I've also discussed being simultaneously subjective and objective—in a sense two people at once. The
objective police officer in you will want to write down
everything to aid his memory—after all, that's what he's
been trained to do. But the subjective bad guy you are portraying simply cannot afford to do this in the presence of
the real-life bad guys.

Do not misinterpret all this. I am not advising you to
not record what happens undercover on paper. Do so at the
first reasonable opportunity, which will usually be after
you have broken cover and are meeting with your surveillance team. In fact, the first thing one of the surveillance
team members should do is hand you a pen and paper so
you can chronicle every detail of what happened. Until this
has been completed, it is wise to not even talk about what
took place, since just as the recollections of eyewitnesses
can influence what each person remembers at the scene of a
crime, discussing the case with members of your surveillance team may accidentally "color" what you remember.

"But," you say, "I'm already carrying a concealed gun,
transmitter, and recorder, so I might as well stick a notebook and pen in my skivvies as well." Why? What earthly
good do you think it will be? Do you plan to whip it out in
the middle of a heroin deal and say, "Excuse me, just need
to record the exact time this buy occurred so I can remember it later on the stand?" The point is, since you cannot
produce your note-taking implements at the scene, you will
be forced to rely on your memory. And since you are forced
to rely on memory anyway, why take the chance of toting
around more cop paraphernalia?

WHY WE REMEMBER SOME THINGS
AND FORGET OTHERS

Getting a little worried now, are you? You say you're
the kind of guy who is introduced to someone at a party,
shakes their hand, and 10 seconds later can't remember

their name? You have to make a list before you go to the grocery store, even if all you need is rice, bananas, apples, and Spam, because if you don't, you'll remember that there were two fruits you needed and one of them was bananas but the other . . . ? Are you having second thoughts about the whole idea of working undercover because you suspect that your bad memory will be even worse, considering the additional stress you'll be under?

Well, relax. A little, anyway. The key to developing a better memory is understanding why you remember some things but forget others, and altering your philosophy a little. The reason we remember things can be summed up in one word: importance.

Importance

Try to remember the last person you met at a party. Did you hear their name and then immediately forget it? Why? If you are honest with yourself, you will say that, either consciously or subconsciously, you did not believe it was particularly important to know that person. You probably thought that you would never see him again, or she was not particularly attractive, or there was nothing he or she could do to help you. (That last one hurts a little, doesn't it?) In any case, you did not consider it important to remember that person's name.

Now, try to remember the last person you met whose name you did remember. There was a reason their name stuck in your mind, and regardless of what that reason was, it made remembering it important. It might have been that during the introduction, you learned that the person was moving into the office down the hall, remembered that the coffee machine is just outside his door, and realized that you'd be seeing him several times a day and you'd have to say hello. Maybe you were introduced to Captain Neely and learned that not only was Neely a captain, he was about to become your new captain. Or maybe the person was a member of the opposite sex who just flat turned you on. The reasons we remember people's names, or anything else for that matter, vary from situation to situation, but one thing remains constant: if you remembered, there was a cause that made it important to remember.

Rewards and Punishments

What creates the importance that makes some things remain in our brains long after other information has fled the gray matter is rewards and negative consequences. If you happen to have a teenage son in your house, think of how many times you've heard his battle cry, "I forgot." (It ranks right up there with "I didn't do it," and "It's not my fault.") But, did he forget to call that foxy-looking girl who just moved to town and sits next to him in English class? Of course not. It was important. Remembering to call meant that she might go out with him Saturday night. Forgetting meant that she wouldn't even have known he existed. And while enough testosterone to kill a man my age was surg-

This young man has forgotten to clean his room. Because he knows your threats of grounding him will not be carried out, his forgetting carries with it no importance or negative consequences. (Photo by Gary Campbell)

ing through his brain, he forgot to clean up his room like you told him to. Why? Because it wasn't important. He would get no reward for remembering to do it, and there would be little or no negative consequences if he forgot.

It turns out that the new girl agreed to go out with him, so he asks to borrow your car. Come Saturday night, you hand him the keys and say, "Be sure to stop at the gas station on your way home. I'm working the graveyard shift tomorrow, and I won't have time to fill it up on the way in."

Did your son remember to fill the gas tank? Of course not. Why? Again, it wasn't important to remember. At the end of his date, he had enough gas to get home. He knew you would not reward him for remembering, and except for your usual look of disgust (big deal), there would be no negative consequences for forgetting. Subconsciously, your teenager knew that you would find time to fill your gas tank yourself, even if you were running late. You would have to get to work, and failure to do so would have negative consequences for you, not him. Also, because he knows that having a full tank of gas in your car is important to you, he knows that the car will have gas in it the next time he needs it.

But let's change the rules of the game on your kid for a minute. Let's give remembering things importance through rewards and negative consequences. Instead of busting your butt to get to the gas station and still make it to work on time, you call your partner, who not only picks you up that night, but agrees to take you to work every night that week. Saturday night rolls around again, and it's time for your son to go pick up that little English class babe for their second date. "Surprise, Junior, the Chevy is still sitting where you left it, and you get to walk four miles to and from the gas station carrying a five-gallon gas can."

Suddenly, forgetting to fill the gas tank has negative consequences, and next time you tell him to fill up the tank before he comes home, he is more likely to remember. But if you really want to make sure he remembers, offer him an incentive for remembering. An extra $10 to take on his date might be the ticket to ensure that you get a few hours of sleep before the graveyard shift begins.

I'm not sure you should listen to me in regard to proper child rearing, but you can take me at my word on this: adults are no different from children when it comes to what we forget and what we remember. We remember things that seem important, and things seem important if we are rewarded for remembering them or punished for forgetting them. Now do you see why you remembered the rice, Spam, and bananas but forgot the apples when you went to the grocery store? It's because you like rice, Spam, and bananas. It was important that you remembered them, because you would be rewarded with eating them if you did, and you would experience the negative consequence of going without dinner if you didn't. But the apples—it's

"Did she say apples or oranges?" In the overall scheme of things, it wasn't important enough to make an impression on your mind. But in undercover work, what seems trivial at the time of the assignment may take on colossal importance by the time the case gets to court. Attach artificial significance to details if necessary. (Photo by Gary Campbell)

your wife who likes apples. You weren't going to get any substantial reward for remembering them, and forgetting them held little consequence (you insensitive S.O.B.).

If you can't remember whether or not a smack dealer you scored from last July was wearing a hat or not, it's because you didn't think you'd get rewarded for remembering, and that there would be no negative consequences for forgetting. And who knows? You might be right. Maybe the defense attorney won't ask you if the defendant was wearing a hat at the time the alleged transaction took place. Maybe when you say you can't remember, he won't turn to the jury with that smile that makes you want to slap him and say, "Special Agent Jones, if you can't even remember whether or not the defendant had on a hat, how can you be sure this is even the same man you say you bought drugs from?"

Artificial Importance

When we forget some bit of information, regardless of how important it may actually be, it's because we didn't consider it important at the time. We've got a lot on our minds already, and most of us have an unconscious resistance to cluttering up our brains with anything we don't think we absolutely need. (This is also known as mental laziness.) So how can we determine what is important to remember when we are undercover? The answer is, we can't. You can never be sure which trivial details will be of paramount importance. Therefore, you must try to remember as much as you possibly can about everything, which requires you to place an artificial importance on some things.

Learn to attach artificial importance to things you may consider unimportant by exaggerating what the rewards for remembering or what the negative consequences for forgetting will be. Then use mental imagery to "see" the results in your mind. (You'll be surprised at how powerful imagery can be and how soon this technique becomes second nature to you.)

For example, when it comes time to go to court, if you can

describe the bad guy's hat as a short-billed, navy blue and cream colored, Cooperstown Collection reproduction of a 1905 Detroit Tigers baseball cap, the jurors will think, "Damn, this guy is good—if he can remember all that, he must remember everything else accurately too." It makes sense that they would think that—it's a logical, ordinary reaction. But you need something out of the ordinary, something really crazy, to help you remember the hat. Imagine the jurors being so impressed with you that they begin to clap. Their applause escalates into a standing ovation, and suddenly a brass band appears in the courtroom and begins to play as the defendant's cap lowers from the ceiling on display. You see it clearly. (It is very important that you *see* it.)

You can also take this exercise in the opposite, negative direction. Imagine that you remember there was a hat of some type keeping the fleas from jumping off the defendant's head, but you can't remember what it looked like. Start out realistically with the jurors thinking, "What a dork. Does he remember *anything*?" Then imagine things escalating. A low murmur starts in the jury box and gradually builds. "Kill him!" one of the jurors yells, "Kill the ignorant undercover monster!" Suddenly, you are being chased through the hallways by jurors carrying torches and pitchforks. The defendant is leading the way, laughing at you, but he is wearing the baseball cap he wore the day you busted him, and you can see it in full detail.

Okay, you thought I'd lost my marbles when I told you to take acting classes and write undercover scenarios using the commedia dell'arte form. Now you're convinced that I've gone bonkers. All I can say is, I didn't invent the concept of using the ridiculous to aid memory; it's a technique most memory experts employ in one form or another. The key is to associate what you want to remember with a scene that is so irrational that it sticks in your brain. Quit worrying about how preposterous this seems right now and try it—it works. You have an imagination and you want results, don't you? Or are you a Homesteader?

Stress

The additional stress under which you find yourself when working undercover, rather than hindering your memory, can actually enhance it. When you go undercover knowing that every aspect of what occurs may be important to both your safety and to the case, your mind becomes more alert and can be trained to focus intensely on details you might otherwise overlook.

Recall an old drug buy you made. Not the first one—it has its own importance and is too easy. Choose a case early in your police career, but after you'd been around long enough for the new to wear off. Do you remember what you were wearing? I do—a Captain Marvel T-shirt, faded blue jeans, and cowboy boots. The bad guy, who had burglarized a drug store in a nearby town, wore a brown plaid shirt, jeans, and cheap blue running shoes. He and I discussed Zap comic books, of all things, as I purchased several vials of Talwin. Why do I remember these details almost 20 years later? Because of the acute state of mind the stress of the situation brought on. Also, I knew that I would need to know them later if the case went to court, and that to not remember could mean that the maggot would go free.

The Finger Method

I learned an extremely valuable memorization technique and a worthy lesson about memory when I was a junior in high school. It didn't take long for me to realize that biology wasn't going to make the endorphins in my brain jump up and dance the hula. But even though it bored me to tears, I knew I needed to pass the tests if I expected to graduate from high school and someday get a job where I didn't have to say, "Paper or plastic?" or "You want fries with that?" So I developed what I thought would be a good system for cheating on the tests. But, it turned out to be a system of memorization that enabled me to get As without cheating.

The morning before the first exam, I opened my textbook and wrote the answers to questions I had been told would be on the test in the webbing between my fingers. The only downside I could see to the system was the possibility that the teacher, who was famous for pacing the aisles during exams to check if people were cheating, would catch me. I knew that each time I glanced between my fingers, I would first have to make sure that she was looking the other way. But I considered the reward of success on the test to outweigh the consequences of failure as the result of getting caught cheating.

The tests were handed out, and I looked at the first question—What is the simplest form of animal consisting of a naked mass of protoplasm?—and an amazing thing happened. In my mind, I saw the word "amoeba" written between the index and middle fingers of my right hand. I didn't need to open my fingers and risk getting caught—I could visualize the word on my skin, scrawled there almost illegibly with my left hand, without looking. So I wrote the word amoeba after question number one and moved on to question number two, which had to do with one-celled reproductive or resistant bodies. This time, I visualized the word "spore" written just above the class ring on my left hand. In my mind's eye, I could even see where the blue "s" had smudged because I'd closed my hand before the ink had dried. I moved on to question three, and by the time the test was over, I'd answered every question without having to open my fingers once.

Why did this work the way it did? I'm no psychologist, but I believe that the knowledge that I might get caught cheating created an interest in the test that amoebas and spores couldn't create on their own. This, combined with the reward and negative consequences factors (reward: an A on the test—negative consequences: "Go tell the principal you were cheating!"), gave me an important reason to remember the answers, which was also supported by the intrigue of playing cloak-and-dagger with my teacher. There was also the stress of the whole situation, which helped focus my mind when I wrote the answers between my fingers. Whatever the process was, it worked. To this day, I cannot think of the word spore without seeing it written between my fingers.

I used this system, which I came to call the "finger method," as a study aid in other high school classes, and in college I developed the ability to visualize the answers to my tests written between my fingers without having to actually write them there. This worked pretty well, but not quite as well as knowing that they were there and that I risked getting caught. (Try explaining to a teacher that yes, you wrote the answers between your fingers, but no, you had no intention of looking at them.) But this makes sense. After all, I had removed the stress factor that had focused my mind so acutely before.

DEVELOPING YOUR ABILITY TO REMEMBER

What does all this have to do with developing your memory for undercover work? A lot. At some time in your life, you have had experiences involving memory that are similar to my finger method. (I like to think of this as the first time I gave a teacher "the finger.") I do not know what your experiences are, but I know they can be used to your advantage when you are unable to jot things down on paper. Remember that you are operating on the theory that everything you see and hear is important. Your reward for remembering details will be that one less sociopathic Neanderthal man will infest the streets. The negative consequence for forgetting will be the possibility of losing the case or embarrassment. So put my finger method or a similar technique of your own to work.

What's that? An example of how you can do this would be helpful here? Okay.

An informant once told me that he could put me onto a guy named Kurt who was selling stolen guns. "How do you know they're stolen?" I asked. He shrugged sheepishly, and it was clear that he only suspected the guns were stolen. The five-man interdepartmental task force I was with at the time worked within a very tight budget, which meant that we could not spend money on guns that might turn out to be legitimate.

I had the informant take me to Kurt's house anyway. My story was that I had friends to whom I could turn the guns over, but before I approached them I wanted to see exactly what he had and what shape they were in. Kurt understood and let me examine each of 14 rifles, pistols, and shotguns.

While Kurt watched me test actions, trigger pulls, and safety mechanisms, I memorized serial numbers by visualizing them being written on the webbing between my fingers. When I finished, I agreed to return the next day with money and a list of what I needed. I left and returned to my office immediately. Out of the 14 weapons I examined, I was able to correctly recall the serial numbers for 11 of them. Of the remaining three serial numbers, I went completely blank on one and transposed digits on the other two, which invalidated them. But 11 were correct, and 10 of them came back as "hits" (stolen) from NCIC—which was more than enough to get a search warrant issued.

I am not the Amazing Kreskin, and there is nothing miraculous about what I did. You are more than capable of doing this and more if you practice this or any other system that helps you remember. The operative word is *practice*. As with anything else, the more you do it, the easier it becomes. Your memory develops like a muscle—the more you use it, the stronger it becomes. There are many helpful books and tapes on the market that present different techniques for memory development. Go to the library and check the card catalogue under memory, or go to your local bookstore and look in the self-help section for books on memory. You can also look under the names of various authors. I'd tell you who they are, but I forgot.

CHAPTER 14

Undercover Weapons

Okay, serious time now. This is the part where I give you advice on how to keep your head from getting blown off with a 12-gauge shotgun while you're working undercover.

It goes without saying that an undercover officer's brain is his best weapon, and that a smoothly run undercover operation that includes a convincing performance by that officer should render other weapons unnecessary. The operative word here is *should*. Murphy's Law follows all cops around, but as soon as you hang your uniform in the closet and start to grow your beard, it seems to become as faithful as the most loyal dope-sniffing K-9.

No matter how well you plan an operation, things can go wrong. This means that unless you don't mind dying, sooner or later you may have to kill someone. When you go undercover, you enter one of the high-risk areas of law enforcement. I know officers get run over directing traffic, but let's face it—you're pretending to be a bad guy, you're hanging out with bad guys, and you're doing illegal business deals with bad guys, and what do bad guys do? They lie, cheat, steal, and hurt people. Granted, you'll be just as dead if some little old lady shoots you while you're writing her a speeding ticket, but the odds of taking a bullet when you're undercover are far greater.

While your first responsibility is to yourself and your partner, you have a secondary obligation to your informant if he's undercover with you. You're a cop, after all, and cops are supposed to "protect and serve." (This doesn't apply to a snitch who sets you up, of course, and he should be made aware at the onset of the operation that if you go down, you're going to take him with you.)

ARM YOURSELF

Never go undercover unarmed, even if you're working a case that seems as nonviolent as shoplifting. Don't listen to any pencil-necked Homesteaders who try to tell you that the bad guys are not dangerous or that you should rely on the surveillance team if anything goes wrong. Rely on yourself. The days when most departments, bureaus, and agencies stood behind their people are over. Although they will never admit it, even to themselves, many administrators would rather you get killed than they get sued. To some of these guys, you are nothing more than a piece of equipment: one of the moving "parts" that make up the department "machine." A lawsuit and bad publicity can bring the machine to a screeching halt, but the parts of the machine are easily replaced.

CHOOSE YOUR WEAPON

For protection, you have your wits, whatever abilities you possess as a hand-to-hand fighter, and whatever weapons you bring along. Those weapons will most likely be guns and knives, but regardless of what instrument you choose, it is like the rest of your undercover ensemble in that it must fit your character. If you are creating the illusion that you are a strung-out heroin junkie, it isn't likely that you'll be toting a Wilson customized Colt .45 with a carry comp. On the other hand, this is exactly the type of weapon a wealthy drug dealer with a legitimate business front and legal concealed carry license might choose.

Regardless of what weapon you carry, remember the rule about it having a story and a reason to be there. For instance, the junkie could have come across the high-dollar customized gun while pilfering a car. With a story, you can cover many of the contradictions that inevitably come up, and a good story will protect you better than any firearm on the market. This doesn't mean that you readily spout out the weapon's history to anyone who asks; bad guys don't readily give up their sources. But play each situation by ear, and have a story ready if the need arises.

Don't Carry "Cop" Weapons

Ideally, you should carry a weapon that fits your character and is not associated with cops, but this is not always possible. Sometimes problems can arise with the narrow-minded bureaucratic sycophants who always seem to climb the political back ladder of the departmental hierarchy. (Would they be . . . Homesteaders?) Occasionally, they land in supervisory positions overseeing undercover operations, and this is where the problems begin. They have never worked undercover and wouldn't have the courage to if given the chance. Therefore, they don't understand the problems that the man undercover encounters. I can illustrate this best by example.

A few years ago, I worked for an agency that will remain nameless, since the vast majority of its officers are hard-working, intelligent, and fearless. Hired to work undercover in the oil fields of the Southwest, I was issued a 4-inch S&W Model 66. Not only was this weapon too bulky for undercover concealment in the summer, at the time there was no gun in the world more closely identified with "the man." To top it all off, the revolver had the agency seal imprinted on the side plate—not a great gun for undercover work.

Okay, Homesteaders love memos, so I "memoed" for another gun, specifically citing my objections to the one I'd been issued. A week later, after the memo had gone up and down the chain of command and been initialed by so many people that the text was unreadable, I was presented with a 2 1/2-inch version of the same gun with the same agency seal.

I launched a new memo campaign, and 10 days later I was given permission to use my own undercover gun as long as it was a .38/.357 S&W, Colt, or Ruger. "These are cop guns," I memoed back. "If I've got to stick to a .38/.357, how about a Taurus or Rossi? Of course I'd prefer an automatic..."

The answer this time was swift. Not only no, but hell no.

Almost a month passed, and I'd been selling allegedly stolen oil to reclaiming plants in reverse stings and buying stolen bits, valves, and other equipment from oil field thieves, who are not always the kindest of people. Many of them like to drink whiskey, use drugs, fight, and shoot at road signs as they race their pickups down the back roads of the oil patch, or, more importantly, at anyone who threatens to end their fun with imprisonment.

While I'd been doing all this, I'd been carrying nothing but a Cold Steel Tanto, because every once in a while these "good old boys" expected me to shoot a road sign or two myself, and I decided that telling them I'd stolen a cop's gun with the agency seal on its side was pushing the story-and-reason-to-be-there theory just a little too far.

The agency and I finally agreed on a Colt Detective Special .38. By then I'd learned that the less they knew the better, so I forgot to mention that I had also decided to carry a Browning Hi-Power 9mm. This was a direct violation of policy, so the .38 would be my primary weapon, and the Browning would be for backup. My reasoning was that if six shots of .38 Special +P didn't do the trick, and I had to resort to the 9mm to save my life, by the time I faced the departmental board of inquiry about my violation of policy, it would seem like nothing more than a bad joke.

Am I telling you to violate your department's policies? No. That's a decision only you can make. What I am telling you is that under specific conditions you may have to decide for yourself whether obeying certain policies is worth risking your life. My feelings are that you should carry what will keep you alive.

I've said this before, but it's worth saying again: regardless of what weapons you have hidden beneath your clothes, the most important thing to remember when working undercover is that you are alone. Forget your surveillance team; even if it's parked right across the street, it'll only get there in time for its members to make good witnesses. This is perhaps the single most important thing for an undercover officer to understand, and it bears repeating even again: you are alone, and you cannot depend on your surveillance team for backup.

KEEP YOUR WEAPON WITH YOU AT ALL TIMES

If you're telling yourself right now that you can probably carry any weapon as long as you keep it hidden, a little further explanation is in order. Bad guys carry weapons, and they like to show them off to each other. They pass them around, compare them, and, to be honest, they're not much different from a bunch of off-duty cops who get together for a few beers at the home of an officer who's just bought a new gun.

Excuse me? You say handing your weapon over for inspection by a guy you're going to bust one day doesn't sound like a bright idea? It isn't. I've never done it, and I don't recommend you to. But handle this situation delicately. If everyone else is carrying and you claim you aren't so that you don't have to "turn loose" of your weapon, the guys with the guns are going to think you're a wimp and you'll lose their respect. They may also decide you're a fool,

Carrying holsters, handcuffs, extra magazine carriers, and a collapsible ASP baton, along with an Aro-Tek LAW 2000 laser sight outfitted Glock 21—a police officer couldn't get much better equipped, but you're trying NOT to look like a cop, remember? Stay away from this stuff when you go undercover. (Photo by Edward Hasbrook)

and it is quite likely that they will rob and kill you. We don't want that now, do we?

This predicament can sometimes be handled by holding your gun up to be seen and explaining briefly that you don't know the present company very well, and you damn sure don't intend to give them your gun. This is a reasonable attitude for a bad guy as well as a cop to have. In any case, good luck. This is only one of the tough decisions you must make in one of the many gray areas you will encounter when undercover.

THE BEST WEAPON IS ONE THAT WORKS

The appearance of whatever weapon you choose need not be pretty—in fact, one with a well-worn finish that any self-respecting cop would be ashamed to have in his holster is perfect. But, like any other piece of equipment on which you stake your life, its function should be flawless.

Over the years, I've carried everything from cheap .22 automatics (weapons that are obtained easily on the street) to a battered Colt M1909 (something that might have been found in Grandpa's old trunk in the attic). What they all had in common, however, is that they worked, and they worked well. Bullets came out of the barrels with the same regularity you get from the most expensive SIG-Sauer or Heckler & Koch, and they struck their targets with the same velocity. I made sure of it by testing them all before I carried them. Well, all but one. Take this story to heart. It could save your life.

One afternoon, I was called unexpectedly at the office and told that an informant had just set up a pretty decent methamphetamine buy and to meet him in 15 minutes. I was dressed okay for the deal, but I was carrying a S&W Model 66 2 1/2-inch .357—about as "cop" as you could get in those days. It just so happened that a deputy sheriff, who was a close friend of mine, walked into the office at that time and pulled out a .380 automatic. He'd picked it up cheaply in one of those gun trades cops are always involved in, thought it would make a perfect undercover gun, and was willing to part with it almost as cheaply as he'd gotten it.

"You shot it yet?" I asked hurriedly.

"Oh sure," my friend said. "It'll take the nuts off a gnat at 20 yards."

I paid him, stuck it in my belt, and went off to buy the speed.

The buy went smoothly, and so did several others over the next two weeks. I began to grow really fond of that little .380—it fit perfectly in my waistband and pockets and was fast into play. Remembering I hadn't fired it yet, I stopped at the range one evening, hung up a target, and pulled the trigger.

"Click."

An investigation of the gun revealed that it had no firing pin. A further investigation revealed that, "Well . . . uh . . . no, Jerry . . . I guess I didn't actually shoot the thing myself . . . but the cop I got it from said he did, and he swore it worked just fine." My friend had even stolen the metaphor about gnat genitalia from this "trustworthy" third party.

Thoroughly test any weapon you will be carrying before you go undercover—yourself.

FIREARMS

Government Model .45s are great undercover weapons. They're big but flat and therefore easily concealable, with unsurpassed one-shot stop potential. Since you are alone, high-capacity 9mms, like the Browning Hi-Power, with the right ammunition are even better. Some of the new high-capacity .45s like those from Para-Ordnance combine the best of both worlds.

Although they are excellent weapons for other areas of police work, Glock, SIG-Sauer, Ruger, S&W, and any other brands commonly seen on the hips of uniformed officers should be avoided. If you prefer revolvers, try Rossi, Taurus, Charter, or any other manufacturer that makes quality firearms but is not as directly associated with law enforcement as S&W, Ruger, and Colt.

Bad guys rarely carry speed loaders or extra magazines, but I've known many to pack more than one piece. If your character and costume permit, you should carry a backup firearm too—.38 snubs and .380 automatics were always my favorites, but the Charter Bulldog .44 is also an excellent choice and offers superior stopping power. The North American Arms mini-revolvers in .22 Short through .22 Magnum are special purpose weapons (sort of like backup backups) and are excellent in the role for which they were designed. I carried one under my shirt on a neck chain for years.

(Clockwise from top) 1) .45 Government Models are hard to beat undercover. This one may be a little too "tricked out" for most assignments. 2) My partner Mark's old Charter Bulldog .44. With the crudely shortened barrel and hammer spur clipped with pipe cutters, it looks like a piece no self-respecting cop would be caught dead with. 3) FEG .380 ACP—copy of the Walther PPK. A good undercover gun, if a little underpowered. 4) S&W 2213—.22 Long Rifle. If you choose something like this, fill it with CCI Stingers and be prepared to shoot a lot, fast. 5) Davis .32-caliber derringer. 6) North American Arms five-shot .22 Magnum. Easily concealed, but, like the S&W and Davis, a better backup weapon than primary weapon. 7) Star Firestar in .45 ACP. Very versatile in undercover roles. 8) Browning Hi-Power. Carries 14 shots of 9mm and is associated more with foreign militaries than cops. (Photo by Edward Hasbrook)

Where To Carry Your Firearm

Detectives and other plainclothesmen fight a constant battle between concealment and accessibility. While the two are not mutually exclusive, they don't go hand in hand either. And when you pose as a criminal, a third element is added to the problem: if the weapon is spotted, it has to look like it belongs to a bad guy, not a cop.

For the most part, holsters are out. The exception is when

you're playing a part like the drug dealer/legitimate businessman who is a crook but has no prior felony record. He also has a legitimate front that could enable him to get the legal licensing to carry a gun, so he doesn't have to worry about getting rid of the piece every time he gets busted for running a stop sign. Ninety-nine percent of bad guys, however, carry guns illegally and are as concerned about ditching their guns as they are about shooting them. Shoulder rigs, or holsters that have to be threaded through the belt, simply don't fit the profile. You might get by with an inside-the-waistband clip model, but to me they still spell C-O-P, and I've never found them to provide much better retention than my belt when the gun is stuck in the right place.

There was a short period (about a week, I think) after concealed-carry fanny packs came on the market that they were used for hiding full-sized revolvers and automatics. Now every plainclothes officer in the free world owns one, and the general public, particularly the outlaw faction, can recognize their pull tabs and Velcro speed openers. If you choose this method of carry undercover, you might as well hang a yellow "caution" sign around your neck that says, "Cop on Board."

This happened with the "safari" or "photojournalist" vest also. For a while they worked fine, but now no one but a cop or a reporter would wear such a thing in temperatures over 72 degrees, and criminals aren't anxious to hang around with guys from either of these professions. Vests are fine for plainclothes work when all you need is medium concealment, but they'll burn you in a heartbeat when spotted by the trained eye of a criminal. If you choose to wear one undercover, buy a cheap one. You won't live long enough to wear it out anyway.

After years of trial and error, I finally decided less was more and settled on carrying a large-frame automatic in my belt beneath my shirt, just in front of my hipbone and in a crossdraw position. I'm a good-sized man, and even under a T-shirt a Government Model or Browning Hi-Power disappears in that position. Lifting my shirttail with my weak hand exposes the grip for a reasonably fast draw, and it has stayed securely in place during numerous scuffles and a couple of out-and-out fights. I ignored the advice of popular gun magazine writers who advise you to buy trousers one size larger in the waist. This is a fine idea if you are trying to accommodate an inside-the-waistband holster under normal plainclothes conditions, but try it without a holster undercover and you will find your gun sliding down your pants leg at the most embarrassing times. Sticking the weapon inside your underwear helps support the gun too; bare skin grips steel better than cotton or nylon. (Remember to clean and oil your gun frequently to prevent it from rusting.) Your belt should be cinched tight to provide extra security.

Yes, this is an uncomfortable way to carry a gun. So what? I hate to be the one to break the news to you, but you can't have everything. You are rarely undercover longer than a few hours anyway, so learn to put up with a little pain. It's a small trade-off for your life.

Keep in mind that this is where I carry my weapon. My gun is secure there for me—not necessarily for you. Where you carry your gun is a personal decision, and your body type and build will have to be taken into consideration. Do some experimenting. Stick the gun where you think you want to carry it, then sprint, jog, and do a few somersaults. You'll find out real fast if you've picked the wrong place.

Women officers have the added advantage, and disadvantage, of purse carry. The good news is that it's easier to stick a gun in your purse. The bad news is it's slower, and the purse is easy to snatch away at a moment when you aren't paying attention.

EDGED WEAPONS

Most officers don't know nearly enough about their firearms, and they usually know even less about other weapons that are perfect for undercover work. I'm thinking of knives in particular. Edged weapons have gotten a bad rap over the years, and the general public associates them only with assassins, street punks, and homicidal maniacs. From a martial arts point of view, this is a shame and reflects our society's increasing tendency to irresponsibly blame inanimate objects for the evil deeds of men. But as an undercover cop who *wants* to look like an assassin, street punk, or homicidal maniac, what more could you ask for than this fallacious assumption?

You should always carry a firearm, but knives make great backup weapons and have three distinct advantages over guns as undercover weapons: 1) criminals do not directly associate them with cops, 2) most (not all) undercover confrontations take place within, or close to, arm's length (knife range) of your attacker, and 3) unless you're stupid enough to throw it, knives never run out of ammunition.

A knife should be carried as a primary weapon only under the most unusual conditions, but to be perfectly honest, if I'm close enough to use a blade, I'd rather have one in my hand than a pistol. Many of the potential problems that plague the pistoleer are nonexistent for the knife fighter. Knife thrusts do not exit their intended target or penetrate walls and kill innocents in the next room. A wild slash or stab with a knife rarely injures the wrong person, and even if it does, the injury is likely to be less severe than the damage a stray bullet can cause. Knives are harder for the bad guys to take away from you, as they are likely to get their fingers cut off trying to do so, and the knife wielder retains control of the lethal portion of his weapon throughout the confrontation—something that cannot be said for the gunman once his bullet leaves the barrel.

Choose a Knife that Fits Your Character's Image

The type of knife you choose is as personal a decision as choosing your firearm. Make sure it fits not only your hand, but the character you are portraying. There are exceptions, but if you choose a fixed blade with a conventional carry system, a 5- to 6-inch blade is usually the practical length to carry. I find the shorter boot knives to be ideal, my personal favorites being the Cold Steel Peacekeeper II, the SOG Pentagon, and a handmade Damascus blade made for me by George Englebretson of Oklahoma City. The Applegate-Fairbairn by Black Jack is a little larger yet easy to conceal with the proper sheath. Bud Nealy of Stroudsburg, Pennsylvania, makes the Multi-Concealment System, a unique knife/sheath arrangement in which the knife is secured with rare earth magnets and can be carried and drawn quickly from a variety of positions. Al Mar, Cold Steel, Blackjack, and other companies also produce excellent boot knives at reasonable prices. (Don't forget the price aspect—if the cops stop you in a car with the bad guys, the criminals will be tossing their weapons out the window, and you will too if you want to preserve your cover.) Make sure the sheath you carry has an open top, or at the very least a thumb break release. Many sheaths use safety retainers that are reminiscent of the old "suicide" gun holsters, and these straps didn't get their nickname by chance.

With a little practice, lock-blade folding knives with thumb studs or similar opening devices can be produced from concealment as fast or faster than fixed blades. Spyderco's CLIPIT "thumbhole" folders are my personal favorites, although I find them easier to open using my index finger rather than my thumb. I have carried various Spyderco models since the Worker first appeared in 1981 and currently alternate between the Police, Endura, and Civilian, depending upon the role I'm playing. Cold Steel, SOG, Al Mar, and other companies also manufacture quality folding knives that fit the bill.

Knives differ from guns in that there is no such thing as a "cop" blade. Even the Spyderco Police model is not automatically associated with law enforcement. Edged weapons are not controlled through serial numbers (some collector edition blades are excepted), BATF "yellow" forms, or other such well-meaning but worthless and sometimes

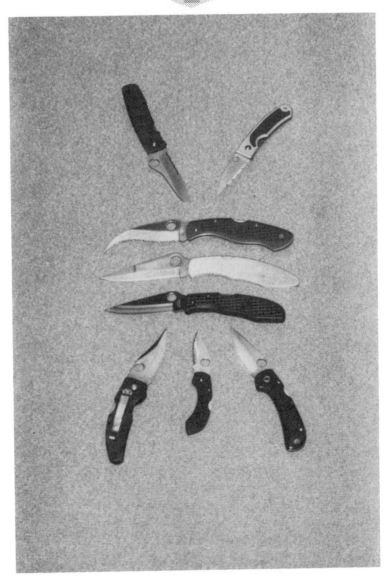

Spyderco's folding knives are quickly drawn and opened with one hand. Top: Terzuola (left) and Centofante (right) models. Center: (top to bottom) Civilian, Police, and Endura. Bottom: (left to right) Black Hawk, Dragonfly (makes an excellent money clip), and Goddard models. (Photo by Edward Hasbrook)

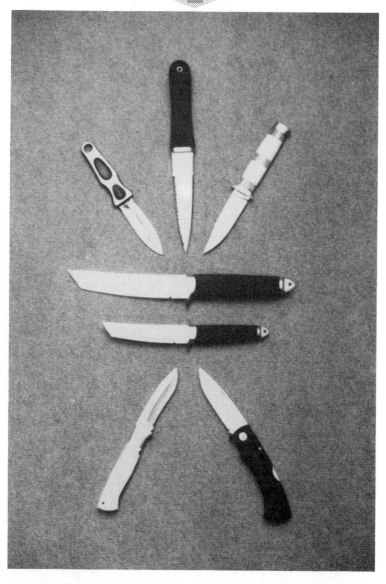

Top: (left to right) A.G. Russel Sting, SOG Pentagon, and a custom-made boot knife by George Englebretson. Center: Cold Steel New Tanto and Mini Tanto. Bottom: Black Jack Mambe (left) and Al Mar (right) folders. (Photo by Edward Hasbrook)

harmful nonsense. Knives are available over the counter with no "paper trail," so convicted felons buy them in stores just like you and I do. This is good news for you, as it means that no knives are too "coppish," and you can carry the best blade that you can afford. I suggest you do. Even the most expensive knives are cheap when compared to life insurance policies.

Training

A good blade and some training at a dojo that teaches tantojitsu, arnis de mano, or any other legitimate knife fighting art make a fine defensive combination in undercover work. Training seminars are conducted every year throughout the country by Dan Inosanto, James Keating, Kelly Worden, and other experts. (Check out some of the knife magazines at your local newsstand.) Master at Arms

Like Crocodile Dundee said, "That's not a knife, THIS is a knife." If you think the Crossada is too big to conceal, wait until you see the unique carry systems it employs. This may well be the ultimate undercover blade. (Sorry, model not included.) (Photo by Edward Hasbrook)

James Keating of Combat Technologies (COMTECH) in Walla Walla, Washington, also produces high-quality videotapes, wooden training knives, and other products—I use them myself and recommend them highly. Keating and bladesmith Bob Dozier have developed an exciting new knife known as the Crossada. Although far larger than I would usually recommend for undercover carry, this amazing blade is available with several unique carry systems that make it feasible to use from the boardroom to the biker bar. One of the most "un-cop-like" weapons you can find, the Crossada is 17 1/2 inches of steel that, when properly employed, will stop an attacker faster than a .44 Magnum.

As with firearms, educate yourself about your department's policy on knives and any other weapon you choose to carry. Then, if you decide to violate those policies, at least you know what you're up against so you can "C.Y.A." (cover your ass).

Where to Carry Edged Weapons

Where you carry your knife or knives is as personal a choice as where you choose to tote your gun: at the belt, under the arm, down the back of the collar—just make sure it's where you can get to it when you need it. If you carry a gun or a knife in your boot with your pants leg over it, you should consider yourself only remotely armed. They'll be picking out the hymns for your service before you get it drawn.

The no-holster theory of undercover guns does not carry over to knives. Even bad guys carry their knives in sheaths. If you stick a bare blade down your pants, bad things will happen to you. (Okay, I know you can figure that out for yourself, but there might be some Homesteaders still with us.) Even shoulder rigs—perhaps the biggest of all no-nos for guns—are acceptable. If the knife has to be ditched, the harness can be cut from under the concealment garment and disposed of in seconds.

OTHER WEAPONS

Sticks and canes are special purpose weapons, and careful consideration should be taken to make sure they fit the character that you are portraying. A slight limp can make the cane believable in almost any role. As with

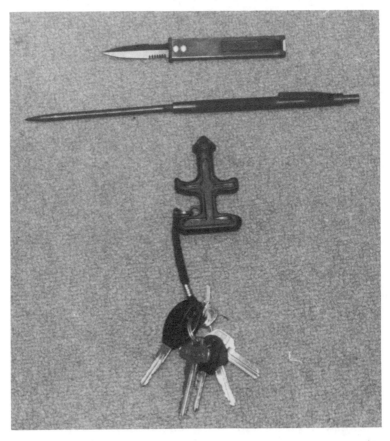

The undercover officer is not overarmed unless it hinders his agility. Backup weapons and even backup backups may come in handy, as long as they don't look like cop equipment. Top: Tekna Micro Knife. Center: Guardian retractable "ball-point pen" spike. Bottom: COMTECH Stinger punching device attached to key ring. (Lose the handcuff key before putting on your beard.) (Photo by Edward Hasbrook)

knives, some instruction is necessary in the use of canes and other impact weapons in order to be able to use them to their full potential.

If you want to become a master at anything, long, hard hours, weeks, and years of practice are inescapable. But becoming competent with a weapon requires far less training than many people think. If you don't have the time or desire to study the art full time, a few hours with a martial arts instructor who teaches Japanese jo or bo, or the Filipino art of kali, and short but regular practice sessions on your own can be beneficial.

Obviously, you want to avoid using weapons like pepper spray, Mace, collapsible batons, and stun guns when pretending to be a bad guy. If I have to explain why, you need to forget about doing undercover work and beg for an immediate transfer to the records division.

Controlling the undercover operation so that weapons are not needed is your best defense, but you should be prepared for unforeseen events by carrying weapons that fit the character you have created, that you feel confident with, and that will do the job. Anyone who has taken even the most rudimentary martial arts course knows that nearly every object in your environment has self-defense potential under the right conditions. So use your head when working undercover. I meant that figuratively, but if you have to, use your head literally, too.

PART 5

TRAPS

The undercover road is paved with more stumbling stones than could be covered in a dozen volumes, let alone one chapter. Each time you put on your beard, you encounter traps that threaten to destroy you, your partners, and even your family and friends. These pitfalls come in every size, shape, and form. Each new trap you encounter is different from the last. You may experience a trap that seems identical to a previous one, but there will always be that "little something" different that makes you unsure exactly how to handle the situation.

Some traps are easy to spot in advance; others appear suddenly with no warning. When you see signs of a trap in your path, proceed just like any other animal in the wild would—step over it, go around it, duck under it, or, if need be, blast your way through it. Those are the easy ones. The ones that may have you chewing off your leg to escape like a coyote in a snare are the traps that you do not see ahead of time. Unexpected traps come from directions you cannot predict and may be set by people on both sides of the law, some of whom you would never suspect of betrayal.

While each trap is unique, they tend to fall into four categories: 1) physical, 2) legal, 3) political, and 4) personal. Failure to recognize, identify, and avoid a physical trap means you may be hurt or killed; fall into a legal trap and you may lose your job and even face criminal charges; the repercussions of political traps range from frozen promotionary status to job loss; and personal traps can crumble marriages and end other personal relationships. Many of these traps are "crossovers" that promise negative consequences in more than one area.

CHAPTER 15
Physical Traps

When I began working undercover in the mid-1970s, even the "mean streets" were "kinder and gentler" than they are now. For the most part, the bad guys didn't carry guns. Even when they did, they did primarily to enhance their image, and they had little intention of using them. I don't mean to say that they wouldn't have hurt you if they found out you were a cop—some would have. But by far the vast majority just wanted to get as far away from you as they could, as fast as they could. They understood that when a cop got killed, every other cop in the world took it personally. It made no difference if the dead officer was a vice cop from Shreveport, Louisiana, the men and women of the NYPD, the agents of the Colorado Bureau of Investigation, and every bobby in London felt like a member of his family had just gone down. You see, there was a real possibility in the "good old days" that when the Shreveport cop killer was finally located in Chicago, Los Angeles, or Baxter Springs, Kansas, he'd be killed resisting arrest. His resistance might not have amounted to much more than an unpleasant look on his face, but the taxpayers of Louisiana would be spared the expenses of his trial, his room and board in the penitentiary, and futile attempts at his rehabilitation.

This was not a particularly bad system if you ask me, and most bad guys didn't want to face heat like that. Unless they were cornered or too stoned to think rationally, they'd go out of their way to avoid hurting a police officer.

But that was then, and this is now.

Talk to any narcotics cop, and he'll tell you that these days, a majority of the bad guys are carrying guns, and their attitude is different. Killing a cop doesn't have the same consequences it used to have. Criminals know they'll go through a lengthy trial, get on TV, write a book, sign a movie contract, and be quite a celebrity by the time they go to the penitentiary—if they go at all. Even if they end up on death row, the appeals last longer than an impotent man attempting sex, and there's always a chance that their attorney can find a loophole, which reminds us how much our justice system has been distorted.

Still, if you get burned undercover, any reasonable bad guy will prefer to just disappear from your sight and memory, but the operative word here is *reasonable*. The unreasonable ones—the brain-dead dopers, the cons who know another felony means life imprisonment, and the true sociopaths—will kill you. That's the good news. The bad news is that the bad guys may think you're an informant instead of a cop.

BEING MISTAKEN FOR A SNITCH

Here the stigma of being a snitch really comes into play, because just as the bad guys know that all the boys in blue take it personally when a cop gets hurt, they also know how cops feel about snitches. They know cops work informants and help them, even though they don't hold them in particularly high regard as human beings, because there is no other way to do their job.

The well-armed bad guys who suddenly surround you inside a dark crack house may have worked as informants themselves in the past. They know that every time cops refer to an informant as "agent" or "operative," they really mean "maggot scumbag snitch." Well, guess what boys and girls? The bad guys think even less of informants than cops do. They have a reason to hate them that you don't have: snitches try to put them in jail. While the bad guys are fully aware that the murder of an informant will be investigated, they also know that the investigation will not be conducted with the same fervor as one for the murder of a cop.

You are far more likely to have serious trouble undercover if they think you are an informant rather than a police officer, but either way, you can die.

WHEN AN INFORMANT SETS YOU UP

Being set up by an informant to be killed or hurt is the first trap that always comes to my mind. This is quite rare, however, if the informant is handled correctly. Even more rare, but hardly unheard of, is an informant setting you up for an assassination that is set to take place while you are not undercover. He simply tells the bad guys who you really are, and they decide to kill you. This is, of course, a possibility that is hardly unique to the undercover man, and from the time you pin on your badge, you should be taking certain security precautions. Do you drive home at the same time every day, using the same route? If so, you are making things easy for someone who wants to set up somewhere along your route with a high-powered rifle.

"Never completely trust an informant" is at the top of the list of undercover rules, and this is one time when you should remember that they are snitches, whether you call them that or not. They do what they do to help themselves, not you, and if they determine that changing horses in midstream will be more beneficial to them personally, they will turn on you with the same enthusiasm they exhibited when they were a member of your team.

Your job, therefore, is to make sure your informants understand that it is safer to be "with you than agin' you," and that betrayal of any sort means there will be hell to pay. Make sure it is clear that even if you are not around to administer the fire and brimstone yourself, your partner or some other cop will be more than happy to do it. The old adage that they need to understand is, "paybacks are a bitch."

This scene appears in countless movies:

A frustrated cop slams his informant against a wall and demands some sort of intelligence that he knows the informant possesses.

"I can't tell you!" the informant always whines. "They'll kill me if I do!"

"And I'll kill you if you don't!" comes the tired old cliché from the lips of the good guy.

So the informant talks. The bottom line is very simple: he can die now or later. It's up to him, and he chooses to stick with the good guy, because dying later beats dying now.

Well, maybe you wouldn't actually kill the informant, but he doesn't need to know this, and it will be good "motivational therapy" if you can, through subtle or perhaps not-so-subtle methods, convince him that you are "badder than the bad" and that it is far safer to be on your side.

If an informant sets you up, or you get burned for any other reason, remember that you are more than likely outnumbered, and do your best to keep the situation from getting out of hand. You may be able to reason with the bad guys, explaining that you are being monitored, and that the entire Dallas Police Department, the Texas National Guard, and a few old Navy SEAL buddies of yours are probably raising their feet to kick the doors in at that moment, but be prepared to face the offenders who have nothing to lose, the crazies, and the ones who panic. You have no way of knowing who they are, so get that ugly blue-worn 1911 Government Model out as quickly as you can. Hope for the best, but prepare for the worst.

FRIEND OR FOE?

Fellow officers and friends can burn you as well. Whether this results from stupidity, honest human error, or out and out malice makes little difference after the fact. You are just as dead if you are set up by another cop who hates your guts as you are if it was simply a, "Whoops, I'm sorry."

Old Friends

Be on the lookout for cops who you went through the academy with six years ago. Sooner or later, the roommate

Sometimes straight cops are the undercover officer's worst enemies. The deputy sheriff about to enter the cafe just recognized you as a friend from Advanced Homicide Training two years ago, and he has no idea you're undercover. The smiles at the table will evaporate as soon as he says hello. (Photo by Edward Hasbrook)

you haven't seen since graduation is going to happen into the bar where you and a guy named Pedro are finalizing the details of a clandestine shipment from Colombia. He may be a fine guy and wouldn't intentionally hurt a fellow officer for the world, but he's been writing speeding tickets since graduation and has no idea what you've been doing. He is, however, delighted to bump into you—it's slap-on-the-back time—and before you know it, he's sitting next to Pedro telling him about the time the two of you found a hole in the wall that led into the female officers' shower room. This will be an honest error, but you (and he) may die because of it. At the very least, Pedro will be selling his coke to someone else.

Gossips

Some officers talk to their wives about their job, and some wives pass that information on to their friends, who tell their friends, who tell their friends . . . This happens with female cops whose husbands can't keep their mouths shut, too. Information spreads even faster if the second party is not a spouse.

Have you ever known an officer who was having an extramarital affair? No? Me either. But for the sake of argument, let's say this impossibility happened. What does a guy do when he's trying to impress a new woman? He tells her how wonderful and exciting he is. If this guy happens to be a cop, he does this by talking about police work, and is there anything more impressive to tell his mistress about than a clandestine operation to which he is privy? Of course not—he's letting her know he trusts her by sharing a secret, and at the same time he's letting her know just how cool he really is. But by the time she tells all her friends, and they tell all their friends, the clandestine operation is no longer clandestine. (I repeat: this happens just as frequently with women cops and big-mouthed husbands or boyfriends spreading their business around.) I'm not sure whether this is a result of human error, stupidity, or both. Regardless, it is food for thought.

Stupidity

Blatant stupidity is more rampant in police work than any of us like to admit. My partner and I were once coerced into going to a small county to make small drug buys for a small sheriff. He had an informant who was in his late teens, and he was sure that together we could "clean up the terrible drug problem" that had coincidentally arisen just a few weeks before the county elections. We met with the informant, who was in the company of a deputy. The deputy appeared nervous. I assumed it was because he had never worked dope before, so I didn't think much more about it. My partner and I were resigned to an evening of wasting our time anyway, and we were committed to getting it over with so we could go back to doing more important things.

The informant took us to a house where we were to purchase one ounce (I told you this was big) of marijuana. A kid about his age answered the door. He was friendly and seemed genuinely sorry when he said, "Gee, I had some but I sold the last bag not 15 minutes ago."

We went to another house, then another, until we finally ended up at a bowling alley, which was the hub of activity for the youths of the village. My partner and I stood out as being at least five years too old and far too "heavy" to be there. After playing a few games of pool, we were convinced that the small county was experiencing the worst marijuana drought in history. So we went back to meet with the deputy.

"You seemed a little nervous earlier," I told the man in the khaki uniform. "Why?"

"Well," he stammered, looking down at the floor. "Uh, maybe I should have told you before. Johnny (the sheriff) gave a talk at the high school this afternoon. He told the kids that he knew some of them were smoking marijuana, but their days were numbered because he had two drug agents coming in tonight to bust them."

Luckily, the sheriff's inconceivable cretinism didn't place us in any danger, because we were dealing with high school kids selling small amounts of marijuana to their friends. I doubt that the thought of trying to hurt us ever even crossed their minds. But I'm sure they had a good laugh at our expense, and I probably laugh harder about it now than they do. The point is that this could have happened with righteous bad guys. For your purposes, don't forget that this sheriff isn't the only complete moron wearing a badge.

Revenge

If you have been a cop for any length of time, you have probably mildly irritated some officers and royally pissed off others. Who are your enemies within your agency? Some you know. Others you suspect. But somewhere in the department there's a guy who has never let on that you offended him. He is lurking behind a smile and an outstretched hand, but even as he insists on picking up the bar tab when the two of you go out for a beer, he is looking for a way to stick it to you the first chance he gets.

If you are working undercover, he will not only get a chance, he will get many of them. Slipping a word to one of his informants, talking a little too loudly at lunch knowing there are interested ears at the next table, making an anonymous phone call to the appropriate bad guys from a phone booth—all of these acts can blow the cases you're working on and put you in physical danger. Never make the mistake of thinking that there aren't cops who would do this to you. They're there, all right. Fortunately, they are the exception rather than the rule, but they are there. It only takes one to put your wife in that insurance line.

Boosting Careers

At the bottom of the food chain is the cop who will risk your life to promote his own. Very early in my career, I was asked to assist a large organization on a heroin case with three members of another task force. I'll call the man who was in charge of the operation "Mike," since I don't think that was the name of anyone involved, and the names must be changed here to protect the guilty. Mike told us that all of his officers were known to these particular dealers, and he needed new faces. Had I not been so young and stupid, I would have realized that Mike had a plethora of officers from which he could draw, and that not all of them could possibly be known. But I wanted to play with the big boys, and I let my ego cloud my judgment.

I began spending many evenings at a certain bar where the heroin dealers hung out with one of the other task force men and an informant. The other two members of the task force pulled surveillance. The informant had been instructed not to rush into introducing us, and, instead, let the dealers get used to seeing us there. About three weeks into the deal, it began to dawn on me that the dealers had seen enough of us, and it was time to fish or cut bait. So I approached Mike and asked him what was going on.

Mike spent a lot of time telling me what a wonderful job we were doing, how well he thought it was going, and how we didn't want to take the chance of blowing it now that we were this close to making a case. But it didn't look to me like we were any closer to a case than the night we'd started, and even a young stupid cop like me was beginning to see that there was something more going on than met the eye.

Before I could figure out exactly what was wrong, however, we were back at the bar that night. Suddenly, I found myself standing back-to-back with my fellow undercover officer. We had our guns drawn but were facing perhaps a dozen other men around the room holding weapons that were aimed our way. As threats were screamed, we gathered up the informant and walked out, still back-to-back. Returning to the apartment where we were staying, we met with Mike and representatives of two other departments who were involved.

"They must have been running countersurveillance," Mike said.

"Maybe they found out the informant got busted and rolled over," one of his mindless little sycophants offered.

More unsatisfactory explanations flew out of the mouths of these "yes men," and it became clear that all who spoke were hiding something, but I didn't know what. All I knew was that the investigation had somehow been compromised, and we might as well pack up and go home. So we did.

Two weeks later, the heroin dealers were busted, and it was a big enough deal to make the news. We learned that a cute little blond we'd often seen at the bar in the company of the main dealer was actually an officer—from Mike's department. (So much for the "we need new faces" ploy.) It took several months for me to put the pieces together, and I still don't know all of the details, but I do know that we were used as decoys so the heroin dealers would have some place to focus their attention while the little blond snuck up and blindsided them. When we began suspecting that something was wrong, Mike decided it was time to pull out his hole card before we got so suspicious that we demanded firmer answers. So between the time I asked Mike why we weren't moving faster and when we went to the bar that night, he burned us—on purpose. And it had the desired effect. The heroin dealers thought the threat was over, and they relaxed. The cute little blond bought dope from them, they went to jail, and Mike became the hero of his organization. And to hell with the fact that fellow cops came close to getting killed, right?

Wrong. What Mike and those who were in league with him did was inexcusable. Had I known they wanted to use us as decoys, it would have been one thing, and I'd probably have let them use me in that manner. But to endanger the lives of fellow officers without alerting them to what's going on is just flat immoral.

Sloppiness

Fellow undercover officers can endanger you in other ways that are not malicious. Several times I had to go under with a man who was my supervisor. He was a self-taught (and self-appointed) undercover expert, but his actions could only be called "fly by the seat of your pants and hope for the best." He made no attempt to control situations in advance and only mildly once he was under. Add to this the fact that the length of his memory was similar to that of an ant's penis, and you are on your way to understanding what a delight he was to work with. Sometimes he forgot to bring the buy money. One time he forgot his gun. He was constantly calling me by my real name in front of the bad guys, and I'd find myself having to resort to lame explanations like, "Jerry is my middle name. He knows I hate it and just calls me that to irritate me." He did have one saving grace, however, and I suspect it was what kept us alive. In the eyes of the bad guys, he appeared far too ridiculous to be a cop.

The physical traps are out there, and I have been able to cover only a few of them. Keep your eyes open at all times. Never let your guard down. Be ready. And if you run across someone like Mike, remember that the game can work both ways. You may decide that the thing to do is hide behind your smile and your outstretched hand, insist on paying all the bar tabs for him, and wait for your chance to even the score. You never know, Mike. That might be exactly what I'm doing.

PERSONAL SECURITY

Taking security precautions is a great idea for anyone these days, but it is especially important for cops, undercover officers in particular. Remember that whoever wants to do you wrong may think you are an informant rather than a cop. Step into their shoes for a moment. How serious do you think the repercussions would be if you broke into the home of an informant (also a bad guy) and beat the hell out of him and his wife? Chances are it wouldn't even be reported to the police, as bad guys often consider being attacked as just an occupational hazard. The criminal who wants to hurt you may be operating from this faulty frame of reference.

Security on the Job

Never eat or drink anything undercover that you don't see come out of the can or bottle and visually follow all the way to your mouth. This is sound advice on paper but impossible to follow in reality. You won't be able to watch the bartender every time he draws you a beer, and you don't know which waitress in the greasy spoon cafe might be hooked up with the bad guy you're about to buy drugs from. But keep in mind that every time something goes into your body while you are undercover, you run the risk of being poisoned or taking a little mental vacation you hadn't planned. More than one undercover officer has suddenly started seeing little blue fairies dance, watching rainbows that included colors he didn't know existed, and had an uncontrollable urge to say, "Wow!" and "Far out!" and "Outta sight!"

Also, do not allow your picture to be taken. Your photograph can get you killed. If this is impossible for some rea-

Did you see the can or bottle opened or the drink mixed? If not, remember that this can always happen. (Photo by Edward Hasbrook)

son, make sure you look as different from your undercover appearance as possible. This sounds easy enough, but sooner or later some well-meaning but ignorant journalist is going to want to do some kind of feature story on you for the local newspaper. The story won't be the problem—you aren't using your real name undercover, and the bad guys know there are spies among them already—but the writer is going to bring along a photographer. We all like to be recognized for what we do, and you're going to be tempted to let him take your picture. Add to this the fact that your Homesteader supervisor says the department needs the good publicity that the story will generate. (The chief is discussing the department's budget with the city council next week, or it's election time for the sheriff.) You'll be facing more pressure here than you suspected, but there are ways to handle this.

One of my fellow undercover officers who was once in this trap had the photographer take an extreme close-up of his face while he was wearing mirrored sunglasses. In the reflection, you could see his gun lying on the desk. It turned out to be just the kind of flash-trash the ambulance-chasing journalist wanted, and the camera was too close to pick up the features of the undercover officer's face. The story was very popular with the public, the department's budget was increased, and my friend threw the mirrored sunglasses that he had never worn anyway into the trash can. Everyone was happy.

Securing Your Home

You may have an unlisted phone number or address, but how hard do you really think it is for someone to get it who is intent on doing so? Your traitorous informant probably has your home phone number already, and he may even know where you, your wife, and the little ones live. If not, simply following you home from work someday will do the trick quite nicely.

That .357 or .45 you keep within reach when you lay

your head down to sleep is worthless if you don't wake up in time to reach for it. And it is worse than useless if some maggot breaks into your house and grabs it before you do.

Your house needs to be equipped with the best security you can afford. This ranges from expensive electronic equipment to strong dead-bolt locks and a good watchdog. Even a small dog that couldn't bite its way out of a paper bag can alert you to intruders. Larger animals, especially when trained, offer not only warnings but protection as well. My Norwegian Elkhound sleeps with one ear on alert and is anxious to feast on anyone he senses does not belong around his family. At the same time, he is so gentle with nonthreatening people that until you have seen him change from Lassie to a timber wolf on methamphetamines, it is impossible to imagine. (Thanks for many years of loyal service, Harpo.)

However unlikely it may be, an attack on you or your family at home is always possible. Dogs can provide both warning and protection. Right now, Harpo is trying to decide whether you are friend or foe. I've seen him work, and I'd advise you to stand real still until he makes up his mind. (Photo by Edward Hasbrook)

If you want a good security system, check around. All metropolitan areas have security companies, and many are operated and often owned by former police officers. These guys miss their work, and they are usually more than happy to give a fellow officer a discount and work out payments that you can live with.

CHAPTER 16

Legal Traps

I have already discussed the grim reality that when you work undercover, you walk a thin line between doing your job as a police officer and breaking the law. In order to create the illusion that you are a bad guy, you must make it appear as though you are doing bad things. If you are not always on your toes, it is very easy to slip across the line and do bad things that are actual felonies.

Every undercover operation is unique, but they all have one thing in common: every time you put on your beard, there is a new assortment of nets above your head and a new collection of snares on the ground. Like snowflakes, no two traps are exactly alike, and attempting to discuss every legal trap that you may encounter would be an exercise in futility. Instead, I'll focus on two ecumenical legal traps: drug use and bribery. Each legal trap you encounter will have its own little twists and turns that make it different enough from the traps described here that you may not catch it if you aren't on guard.

You may find yourself committing a few technical misdemeanors in order to establish your identity as a bad guy. Even a seemingly minor thing like driving with an open alcoholic beverage container in your vehicle may come back to haunt you in court. (Photo by Edward Hasbrook)

DRUG USE

One of the first things most young officers inquire about is their use of drugs when working undercover. Many are worried that they will have to partake in the use of illegal substances in order to authenticate their character. (Although some officers I know appeared to look forward to it.) The answer is simple: don't do it. Putting that answer into practice, however, is where the complications arise.

Just Say No

As I've already said, the larger the drug deal, the easier it is to avoid using drugs. If you are buying a large quantity of an illegal substance, it is more likely that the dealer will assume that you are going to resell it. Therefore, you are tagged as a dealer, and you may or may not also be a user. The only problem that is likely to arise under these circumstances is that the dealer will expect you to sample the product before the buy. Again, don't do it. Instead of sampling the drug, test it. Pull out your little drug-testing kit, just as any smart dealer would, and watch the testing solution change colors. Remember, this is not TV. You do not snort a line of coke and then look up and say, "Hey, not bad—obviously 87.32 percent pure. I'll take all you've got." It just doesn't work that way, and besides breaking the law, you'd be taking a dangerous risk.

The effects of illegal street drugs influence the behavior and thinking of even the practiced user (after all, that's the whole point, isn't it?), and since you are not experienced with the drug's effects (I assume), your abilities will suffer to an even greater degree. In addition, you don't know what the drug was cut with, and you can't even be certain what the drug really is. Sure, the bad guy agreed to sell you heroin, or cocaine, or whatever, but how can you be sure that's what he sets in front of you? Don't do it. Violate this rule, and you may make a mistake from which you won't wake up.

Have a Story and a Reason to Be There

Your story is that you are a drug dealer. Your reason to be there is to buy drugs for resale—not to party with the guy who is selling them to you. Drug dealers don't trust each other any more than they do cops. When the guy who says he's from Medallin holds the little spoon in front of your nose, it makes perfect sense for you to say, "Look, Jose, we don't know each other, and for all I do know, you could be planning to poison my ass and rip me off. We'll toot a little some other time, after I trust you. Right now, we're doing business."

This situation gets more difficult to control the lower you go on the drug chain. In other words, if you go to someone's home to buy an ounce of marijuana, they assume that you will smoke it yourself or share it with your friends. No reasonable human being, with the exception of kids and penitentiary inmates, buys one ounce of grass and then rolls it into joints for resale. If your purchase is small, it is assumed that you are a user, and if the dealer is the friendly sort, it is very likely that he will ask you to join the party.

Simulating Smoking

You're sitting on the dealer's couch and the joint is making its way closer to you. What do you do? In the old days, we used to simulate smoking, but to be honest with you, simulation sucks, and I don't mean that as a pun. To simulate smoking, you pinch the end of the joint tightly, hold it between your lips, and pretend to smoke. It sounds great when they teach it to you in narc school, but it doesn't work too well in the field. Any doper with an IQ one point over that of an average rock can tell you're faking it if they watch closely, and if they have even the tiniest misgiving about you, they will watch closely. That's the downside.

The upside, if there must be one, is that you are not breaking the law by simulating. But if any smoke enters your mouth, sinuses, eyes, or ears, you have ingested marijuana. "What if it is just an accident?" you ask. "Doesn't intent have to be present when you commit a crime?" You're walking a thin line here. What do you think a jury's reaction will be when you tell them that you accepted a lit cigarette that you believed contained marijuana, held it to your mouth, and sucked in, but got none of the smoke into your system? You'll sound a lot like a certain president who told the American public that he "smoked marijuana but didn't inhale." Did anyone, even those who went ahead and voted for him, buy that?

Perjury

Accidentally ingesting marijuana may not seem like such a big deal, but when you're sitting on the witness stand, the defense attorney is going to have a field day. When he asks you if you smoked marijuana with the defendant, all these little details suddenly take on a new importance. You have to decide how to answer this question, but there are a few things you need to consider before you do.

When you think back on it, you suddenly remember that little wisp of smoke that snuck up your left nostril from the lit end of the joint while you were pinching off the other end. You remember that you thought it had to be pretty good stuff, because even that tiny bit gave you a slight buzz. Sure, it was just an accident, but it happened. And there's even a name for that type of marijuana ingestion—"nose hitting."

Then you remember the other time you were at the defendant's house, and they were out of papers so they passed around a pipe. You found out that pinching the stem on a pipe doesn't work too well, didn't you? So you planned on taking the pipe and just clamping your teeth down over the end, then passing it on. But somebody was watching you when your turn came, and since you didn't want to get burned, you had to actually smoke a little. Not very much—in fact, the THC content must have been low because you didn't even get a buzz. But this time, there's no question about it being an accident. You smoked marijuana, and you did it on purpose so you wouldn't get burned.

So, when the defense attorney glances at the jury, then turns to you and asks, "Officer McNiel, did you or did you not smoke marijuana out of a pipe with the defendant on the night of October 15th?" you have a problem. You will have to either say yes, and then listen to him tell the jurors that you are no better than the defendant during his closing argument, or perjure yourself and say no.

Do not take this perjury thing lightly. Oh, it won't be proven that you were lying and you won't go to jail, but you will know that you lied under oath, and you already know from life experiences that telling a little lie is the first step toward telling big lies. We all know criminals lie under oath; they are animals, and it's expected. You are supposed to be one of the good guys, however, and you shouldn't forget it. It's what separates us from the animals.

Have a Story and a Reason to Get Out of There

Simulating smoking a joint is easy compared to creating the illusion that you are using other drugs. Let's see you simulate smoking hash out of a bong pipe. How are you going to simulate tying off and injecting a vein with heroin? I'd like to see you simulate snorting coke sometime. Someone will say, "You know big guy, I saw you stick the straw in your nose, and I saw you sniff. I just can't figure out why that line of white powder is still on the table."

The best way to handle drug use undercover is to stay out of situations where it is expected. While this is often easier said than done, a little planning can shift the odds of pulling it off in your favor. If you are making small user-sized buys, you not only need a story and a reason to be there, you need a reason to get out of there as well—one that the bad guys can understand and identify with. In other words, you need a reason to just do business and leave that would make them want to do the same thing if they were in your shoes.

I often arrived at a buy scene with the story that I wanted to score because I had a woman waiting for me. We wanted to "get high and get nasty"—simple as that. There are a few things dopers have in common with humans, and one is that most of them like sex. The fact is that they probably don't get much of it, at least from a desirable source. (You've seen the personal hygiene of the average small-time drug dealer; you don't think it's Michelle Pfeiffer sneaking through his bedroom window every night, do you?) The bottom line is that getting high and getting laid beats the hell out of getting high and not getting laid, so they'll understand why you're in a hurry to get out of there. But if you tell people of this caliber that you have to hurry so you can visit your grandmother in the nursing home, the significance of the reason for your departure will be lost on them.

Using drugs undercover can have more serious consequences than affecting your courtroom testimony, but I'll get into them in the chapter on personal traps.

BRIBERY

Bribery or graft—call it what you will—like perjury it can sneak up on you a little bit at a time.

Returning Favors

When you were a uniformed officer, honest merchants probably offered you discounts on everything from clothing to automobiles. "You guys don't make enough money for what you do," they told you, or, "I just want to show my appreciation," or maybe it wasn't even that direct. Maybe the fact that you are a police officer was never mentioned.

Bill of Bill's Men's Wear may have cornered you one day and said, "Hey, Jack. I'm overstocked on leather jackets this year and can't sell them all. How about taking one off my hands at cost?" You may have taken advantage of the opportunity Bill gave you, and you may not have. I'm not here to judge you one way or the other. But do you remember who Bill called when he got a speeding ticket recently? Right—you. He didn't come right out and ask you if you could "fix" it; he just asked what you thought he should do. You felt a little uncomfortable, though, when you told him that the easiest thing would be for him to just mail a check to the city clerk's office. That's because you were wearing the leather jacket he sold you at cost when he called.

Even if you did take care of Bill's ticket, it may not seem like such a big deal. Certainly it is not on the short list for the Police Corruption Award of the Century. You might well have "fixed" the ticket of an otherwise sound citizen such as Bill even if he hadn't given you a break on the jacket. (The Homesteaders are screaming at the top of their lungs now. Not that they wouldn't do such a thing for a friend, but they'd never have the courage to admit it!) I'm not trying to draw the line on exactly where friendly gestures end and bribery begins. But even though bending the rules in some cases is a small thing, when you do you enter another gray area that will grow darker if you remain in it.

Monetary Bribes

Working undercover, particularly in the area of drugs, means dealing with people who obtain money illegally. Eventually, someone will have enough illegally obtained money to be able to offer you some if you'll just look the other way. If you've busted them, it will be worth even more for you to "misplace" evidence or do something else that increases the odds against them being convicted. They will never say, "I'll give you five grand if we can just forget this whole thing." Instead, they will handle it just like Bill did—in a roundabout manner that let's you know they are willing if you are but that leaves the proposal too vague to file attempted bribery charges.

Yes, yes, yes. I know you are far above even considering doing something so dishonest. Some of you are even offended that I have suggested that you might consider doing something so dishonorable. That's because at this point in your life, even though you live pretty much hand-to-mouth on a cop's salary, you are able to make the house and car payments, put bologna on the table, and meet the other expenses of existence. Right now, it's easy to "just say no." So let's change your situation a little to help you understand.

You pick up the mail on your way home, and after you flop down on the couch, the first things you open are the Visa, Mastercard, and Discover statements. You finally face the fact that you are approaching your limit on all three. The solemn promise you made to yourself that you would make only the minimum payment for just two months, until you could square the family budget again after buying the new washer and dryer, has suddenly turned into two years. You're wondering if you've got enough credit left to buy your daughter the prom dress you promised.

While you're looking at the bills, the phone rings. It's the mechanic at the garage where you left your car yesterday. He's sorry, but somebody ran the thing low on oil and you're going to need a brand new engine. No sooner do you hang up and it rings again. It's your son, and the

It's easy to avoid corruption when times are good and it comes at you head on. Beware the day when you can no longer pay the electric bill and graft sneaks up on you a little at a time. (Photo by Edward Hasbrook)

university finance officer wants to know why his tuition hasn't been paid this semester. You've got until Friday, after which they'll drop Junior from the roll. This reminds you that you've also neglected to pay his room and board fee at the dormitory.

While you're at it, don't forget that the doctor just diagnosed your younger son with diabetes. Little Timmy is going to be racking up his share of medical expenses. Since you're still trying to pay off your knee surgery, you know that the insurance company picks up 75 percent of all allowable claims, but that "allowable" really means "anything we can't weasel out of."

As you contemplate all this good fortune, you hear the familiar sound of the garage door opening, and the almost equally familiar sound of the electronic opener breaking again. You hear your wife walk in and you look up in time to hear her announce that the company she works for has just gone bankrupt. There goes half of your monthly income. It has not been a good day, and you are not a happy camper.

So you escape into your work that night, concentrating on the cocaine buy you're about to make, as you should. There is something vaguely familiar about the dealer, but you can't place him, and you chalk it up to a slight case of paranoia brought on by the pressures at home. The buy goes smoothly.

The next morning you find yourself sitting outside the office of a new loan officer at your bank. You're wearing your gray "court" suit, and your mission is twofold: you need to stall him on next month's car payment and at the same time talk him out of enough cash to keep Junior in school. The receptionist's intercom buzzes and you hear her say, "Mr. Jackson, there's a Detective Goodpasture waiting to see you about a loan." A moment later, she smiles and tells you to go right in. You smile back as you open the door, because even in the midst of your world exploding, you know that life is full of funny coincidences—this loan officer has the same last name as the dealer you bought coke from a few hours ago. It doesn't seem quite as funny once you're inside the office. It's even less funny to Loan Officer Jackie Jackson. He's standing open-mouthed with his hand extended across the desk, and you realize that not only does he have the same name as the coke dealer, he *is* the coke dealer.

An uneasy silence fills the room as you sit down. Neither of you is sure where you stand. Both of you are in shock and trying to pretend that the other one hasn't recognized you. So you start trying to do exactly what you came to do—get more time to pay your car payment and convince him to trust you with a short-term loan. Jackson's expression begins to lighten a little as he realizes you are here as a customer and don't plan to take him out wearing handcuffs—at least not today. He's not stupid, though. He knows that he sold you a gram of coke last night, and that one day you will be knocking on his door with an arrest warrant. But while all this is going through his cocaine-elevated brain, he begins to understand that you need him.

"Perhaps we can do business," Mr. Jackson says.

He makes it clear that he will allow you to postpone a month or two of car payments if last night is forgotten . In addition, he will fix you up with a new loan that will not only cover the university costs, but will pay off your credit cards and keep you from losing your house, your car, and, in general, your entire life. Oh, one more thing. Jackson's secretary Sally is resigning to have her baby. Your wife has typing experience, doesn't she?

You should refuse, of course, but considering your personal situation, you are going to think—if only for a second—about taking Loan Officer Jackson up on this offer. And if you think about it much longer than that, a remarkable psychological process is going to start to work in your brain. That process is called rationalization; none of us are exempt from it, and in this case it will happen something like this:

Jackie (by now you and Mr. Jackson are on a first-name basis) didn't sell you all that much cocaine—just one tiny gram, and you didn't see anybody else buying anything at the house while you were there. If Jackie's a dealer, he isn't a very big dealer. It seems more likely that he just had a little coke for his own personal use and, since he and the informant are so tight, was willing to share some with a mutual friend.

Posted on Jackie's wall are documents stating that he was once president of the Lions Club, and that he raises funds every year for the United Way. Hell, Jackie is a good citizen, really. He just likes a little toot now and then. Well, who doesn't have something in their life that they have to hide? Lord knows you drink too much sometimes, don't you? Are you going to be the one to cast the first stone?

Then you start thinking, if you are thrown out on the streets, you aren't going to be able to concentrate on your job anymore. It'll affect your attitude, and you won't make good cases and take the real dealers out. Your mind will be on your personal problems, and you might screw up and get some other officer killed. And don't forget your family. Is it right for your wife and kids to suffer because you let financial problems get out of hand?

Before you know it you have signed the loan agreement and are walking out the door. Your rationalizations have even convinced you that you did the right thing. You had to lose the battle to win the war, but a greater good will come from all of it. Your innocent family won't suffer, a good citizen who made a mistake won't go to jail, and if you had to bend the rules a little to accomplish all that, well, that's life. You are still 100 percent against bribery, and you feel that any cop who'd succumb to it ought to be fired, if not shot. But this was a special situation. At least you're right about that—it was a special situation, but only because it involved you.

CHAPTER 17

Political Traps

In Chapter 15, I talked about two things that merit repeating here. First, many traps are crossovers and exhibit characteristics from more than one of the four categories of traps. Second, no matter how great a guy you think you are, you have enemies within your department, agency, or bureau. I'm going to delve a little deeper into these two areas here.

GOOD COP, BAD COP

Remember Mike? Mike wasn't my enemy before the incident I described earlier occurred. We worked for different agencies and hardly even knew each other. Mike didn't set up me and the other task force members because he wished us harm; he just wanted to make himself look good. He wanted to bust those heroin dealers bad, and if officers he didn't know got hurt along the way . . . well, too bad.

But, this would have been a perfect situation for Mike had he desired harm to befall us. He could have leaked additional false information to the bad guys—something along the lines that we already had a good case that we could file on them, or that we were planning to set them up. This would have encouraged the heroin dealers to take more decisive action than threatening us with guns as we made our way out of the bar back-to-back with our weapons drawn.

I hope I'm not giving you the impression that I think every one of your fellow cops is out to get you killed. Luckily, occurrences like these are few and far between. But a sad fact of life is that these things do happen occasionally, and it only takes once to force your wife into that insurance line.

PERSONAL VENDETTAS

I once inadvertently offended a supervisor of mine I'll

Someone you work with may be jealous of your freedom or angry at you for other reasons. They'll be watching . . . (Photo by Edward Hasbrook)

... and maybe even taking notes. Here is a "book" in progress. Forget the fact that the undercover officer asleep at his desk worked 36 hours straight and didn't go home last night. The book will conveniently leave that out and just reflect that he dozed off in the afternoon. (Photo by Edward Hasbrook)

call "Bob Bishop." I didn't know how I'd done it at the time, but when I came into the office one morning, Bob's attitude toward me had changed. To put it bluntly, it was obvious that a man I had believed to be my friend wasn't anymore. The situation escalated, and soon Bob was using his supervisory position to do everything he could to make things hard on me. If he learned that I had something planned with my family, he'd call and send me off on the most ridiculous assignments imaginable. He'd return my reports to be rewritten for any bureaucratic pretension he could come up with, and the most important thing in the world suddenly became that my departmental vehicle be kept spotlessly clean. Soon, he began keeping a "book" on me.

"Book" Keeping

Some of you may be familiar with keeping books. For those of you who aren't, it is something someone who is out to get you does to document your activities, adding to the record their own little interpretations about what you've done. For instance, you might have to interview a witness in a city 100 miles from your office. You go to the subject's home, but when you arrive there his wife tells you he went fishing at a lake that is 50 miles farther down the road. She gives you directions to his favorite fishing area, you drive on, find him, do the interview there, and come home. This is not quite the way it will be presented in a book.

It could just as easily be a co-worker who keeps a book on you, but for the sake of example, let's stick with it being your supervisor. I'll call him Williams, you are Smith, and the witness you went to interview is Johnson. Williams documents your trip to interview Johnson like this:

10/26/95

0815 hrs: Investigator Smith stated to Supervisor Williams that he was about to depart for Cozy Corners, New Mexico, where he planned to interview John Johnson in regard to an ongoing investigation. Investigator Smith also stated that he considered the interview to be "an exercise in futility" because he suspected we would never obtain sufficient evidence to file the case in question. Smith appeared to Williams, however, to be in unusually good spirits.

0817 hrs: Supervisor Williams went to the parking lot and noted the mileage on Smith's agency vehicle at 26,452.9 miles.

0826 hrs: Supervisor Williams passed Smith on his way back into the building. Smith stated that he would be stopping at the Cozy Corners Police Department to get directions to Johnson's home before driving on to the interview. Williams then observed Smith depart in his agency vehicle and noted that Smith turned east as he left the parking lot. Cozy Corners, New Mexico, lies approximately 100 miles west of the agency offices.

1537 hrs: Supervisor Williams attempted to establish radio contact with Investigator Smith but received no reply. He then telephonically contacted Cozy Corners' Police Chief Richard Jones. Neither Jones nor any of his officers had been contacted by Investigator Smith.

1655 hrs: Williams again attempted to contact Smith via radio and the Cozy Corners Police Department telephonically with the same results.

10/27/95

0805 hrs: Investigator Smith arrived at the agency offices. Supervisor Williams then proceeded to the parking lot and noted that the odometer on Smith's agency vehicle read 26,765.4 miles.

0824 hrs: Supervisor Williams asked Investigator Smith if the interview had been successful. Smith replied in the affirmative and stated that he was about to type his report. He also stated that while the subject had been cooperative, it still appeared doubtful that there would be sufficient evidence to file the case. Williams observed that Smith appeared nervous during this conversation.

Summary/Conclusion: The exact distance between the agency offices and Cozy Corners, New Mexico, is 104 miles, making the round-trip 208 miles. Investigator Smith's mileage for 10/26/95 reflects that he drove 311.5 miles, leaving 103.5 miles unaccounted for. Williams observed Smith turn in the opposite direction of Cozy Corners upon leaving the parking lot on the morning in question. Smith did not contact the Cozy Corners Police Department as he had stated he would.

Supervisor Williams is aware that Investigator Smith has a girlfriend in Little Bend, Texas, approximately 150 miles east of the agency offices. It is Williams' conclusion that Smith lied about his activities on 10/26/95, and that he faked the interview report on the assumption that the case would never actually be filed. Supervisor Williams also concludes that Smith went to visit his girlfriend instead of doing the interview, using an agency vehicle and fuel for his personal benefit. This trip would account for the additional mileage.

How Do You Plead?

According to Mark Twain, there are three kinds of lies: lies, damn lies, and statistics. Twain was right, but it's amazing how many people will believe something just because someone else took the trouble to write it down.

Homesteaders in particular dearly love documentation, and it's to a Homesteader that someone keeping a book on you is going to go—as soon as he thinks he's got enough twisted evidence to get you fired, or at least reprimanded.

As you can see, Williams not only put the spin he wanted on the details of his entries, he added lots of other little details that can be neither proven nor disproven. You probably did say that you didn't think the case would ever be filed (after all, haven't you been forced to pursue cases in the past that you knew weren't heading anywhere?), but you made this statement because it was true, not to cover your butt while you snuck off to see your girlfriend.

You also stated that you planned to get directions to Johnson's house at the Cozy Corners Police Department, but you never showed up there. Why? Because the address you had was 1414 Barclay Avenue, and you drove past Barclay Avenue on your way to the police department. You had to conduct an interview and make a 200-mile round-trip in one day, so it didn't make much sense to waste your time shooting the breeze with the boys in blue when Johnson's house practically dropped in your lap. Good thing, too, because Johnson wasn't home, and you had an extra hundred miles to drive to and from the lake, but how are you going to prove this? And while we're at it, how are you going to prove that you turned east out of the parking lot because you decided to grab a cup of coffee for the road at the convenience store on the corner?

Think about this long and hard. Sure, either Johnson or his wife or both of them can vouch that you were in Cozy Corners—if they choose to cooperate. But this will be embarrassing at best ("My chief doesn't believe me, Mr. Johnson. Could you please save my job?"), and there's no guarantee that they'll even agree to get involved in a departmental problem. It could be worse, though. Let's change the details a little and see where you stand.

When you arrived at Johnson's house, instead of his

wife, you found a note stuck in the door that read, "Honey, gone fishin' at Lake Sock-It-To-You. Be back later." You drove all over the lake area but never found Johnson, so you came back empty-handed and no one saw you the entire day.

This is just one incident. Consider the fact that Williams has been keeping his book on you for a month, or six months, or even a year. He's got hundreds of twisted episodes written down on paper, and by the time you get to the review board, most of them will be only vague memories in your brain. There will be no way to prove that you are not guilty of what his paperwork reflects, and if you've ever gone before a board like this, you know it is not a court of law. The burden of proof will be on you; you are guilty until proven innocent. Add to all this the fact that there may be a few minor departmental policy infractions of which you really are guilty, and you can readily see that you'll be descending quickly through Dante's Nine Circles of Hell.

Revenge

Returning to Bob Bishop and me, what had I done to offend my supervisor? I didn't have the foggiest notion. When I finally asked him, he acted surprised and said nothing. Then he went right back to making my life as miserable as he could.

I didn't find out the truth until years later, long after I was no longer employed by the department for which Bishop worked. Finally, I learned from his secretary that I had made a friendly joke one day while the three of us were having lunch together. Only a bizarre mind such as Bishop's could have stretched the remark into an insult, but that's how he took it. The misunderstood statement embarrassed him in front of his secretary—a woman who played a starring role in his sexual fantasies—and rather than confront me as any honorable person would have done, he took the cowardly approach of getting revenge.

Jealousy

Undercover work gives the officer far more freedom than most other areas of law enforcement. This drives Homesteaders crazy, since they assume that if they are not breathing down your neck all the time, you will do something stupid or dishonest, or you will just screw off. They will watch you as closely as possible because it is their nature to do so. Your freedom may promote jealousy in other officers also—even fellow Explorers—and this is another reason someone may try to put you in the "trick bag."

In the end, the reason a fellow cop tries to get you reprimanded, dismissed, or even killed is of little importance. The important thing to remember is that some are capable of such dastardly behavior. You should be ready for whatever traps their devious little minds can come up with. No matter where you work, there are Bob Bishops and Mikes somewhere close by.

CHAPTER 18

Personal Traps

Personal traps are just what they imply: traps that have an adverse effect on your personal life. Granted, traps that result in unemployment or imprisonment can put a strain on your family situation, but entanglements resulting from personal traps can end your marriage and make sure your kids grow up calling somebody else Daddy. The vast majority of personal traps involve elements in three broad categories: drugs, alcohol, and sex.

DRUG ABUSE

When I first pinned on a badge, the only investigation conducted on me was a background check to ascertain whether or not I had a felony record. (By now, I've probably convinced you that if there had been one, I wouldn't have gotten the job.) Nowadays, the applicants for most departments are more carefully screened, and uncovering any use of illegal substances is invariably a top priority. There are several reasons for this.

Skeletons in Your Closet

Since the Homesteaders who often run the show have an anal-retentive obsession to organize things into neat little categories, they can't believe that anyone who ever smoked a few joints in high school isn't still doing so. To them, you're either a doper or you're not, and if you ever were, you still must be. They are quick to suspect, however, that an officer who was clean before going undercover began using drugs afterward. They believe that people can change—but not for the better. So Homesteaders are usually in favor of systematically eliminating all police applicants with any former drug use—with no exceptions.

Any department that follows such a policy is robbing itself of many potentially excellent officers, and I'll discuss why a little later. But for now, I confess that there are reasonable questions that must be answered concerning drug use by a potential officer. For example, with which types of drugs did the candidate experiment? Did his experience stay within the realm of experimentation or escalate into use? And, most importantly, is the candidate still using? How the answers to these questions are interpreted requires some explanation before I move on.

Taming the Tiger Within

The inherent spirit of adventure that all Explorers possess is both a blessing and a curse. There are few constructive vents for its expression prior to adulthood. Sports and other activities help, but they only go so far. Since Explorers love the thrill that accompanies danger, and the easiest way for a young Explorer to experience that thrill is to break the law, most of them do at one time or another. They are usually minor infractions, and most often the young Explorer grows out of them as he matures and finds other avenues to explore. Those who do not and continue to break more serious laws after reaching adulthood are called criminals. But some adult Explorers redirect their adventure drive into more socially acceptable channels, and these people are called cops. Often, they are the best cops around.

In other words, the same spirit of adventure that leads someone to choose law enforcement as a career may have led to a little drug experimentation when they were younger. The constructive Explorer will give drugs (probably marijuana) a try, recognize the destructive potential both physically and legally, and then give it up. As with all things, there are exceptions.

Dear Prudence

"George" was a drug dealer in high school. He avoided a citywide bust by the skin of his teeth, had a dramatic change of heart, and stopped. A few years later, he applied for a position as a deputy sheriff. Since he had no arrest record, and the department did not impose preemployment polygraph testing, he was was hired and assigned to work in the narcotics division. I worked with him off and on for almost four years, and he was possibly the best undercover operative I've ever known. He fully understood both sides of the game and could think like a drug dealer as well as he could a cop. He was scrupulously honest, never used drugs undercover or at any other time, and did nothing that could give the Homesteaders a reason to not hire men like him.

On the other side of the coin are former users who want to be cops but are still using or are susceptible to starting again. This cannot be tolerated. But even with the extensive use of polygraphs, psychological testing, and background investigations, a few bad apples still sneak through the Minnesota Multiphasic Personality Inventory (MMPI) and enter the barrel. I have known a few undercover officers who simply defected to the other side. They began hanging around with dopers, decided the other team was having more fun, and were suddenly gone.

Most people have the prudence to know that the pleasure and amusement attached to drug use is fleeting, but it is a reality, at least in the beginning, or no one would use illegal drugs to begin with. Because of this and the fact that you will be exposed to these substances more than anyone else legally, you must pledge that you will not use drugs undercover under any circumstances.

ALCOHOL ABUSE

"Someday you'll drown in a vat of whiskey," someone said in a W.C. Fields movie.

"Ah, a vat of whiskey," Fields replied. "Death where is thy sting?"

Well, the sting is there waiting for you when you begin an undercover career. Most of you are already aware of the fact that law enforcement officers have one of the highest alcoholism rates of any profession. I'm not aware of any studies done specifically on undercover cops, but from what I've seen, I'd guess it's even higher.

Drinking Undercover

Undercover work often entails drinking. You meet bad guys in bars, or you go to their homes or motel rooms, and everyone downs a few. More often than not, a few too many. How drunkenness is viewed depends to a large degree on the level of society you are working with. Remember the cocaine-dealing banker, Mr. Jackson? That's right, the one who gave you the loan. Getting rip-snorting drunk at his next Christmas party and throwing up all over Mrs. Jackson will not be viewed as proper behavior. Just the same, if you find yourself in a biker bar waiting for a Hell's Angel named Horsemeat to bring you a load of crank, ordering a Perrier with a twist is likely to be viewed as equally deviant behavior. As in all other aspects of undercover work, your drinking deportment must fit both your character and the environment. And while you're making it fit, you've got to try not to turn into a lush.

Determining Whether You Should Drink

If you even suspect that you have a drinking problem, stay away from undercover work. If you are already working undercover and think you are developing a problem, get away from it. I am not pretending to be an expert in the field of alcohol abuse. I do like to think, however, that God gave me at least a modicum of common sense, and I know what I have seen. Anyone who already has a problem with alcohol is very likely to see that problem escalate. People who don't realize they carry whatever yet-to-be-identified gene that causes the disease sometimes discover they do.

It is not impossible to work undercover without drinking, but it's damn hard, and I've known only a few officers who pulled it off. One older man, a recovering alcoholic who religiously attended Alcoholics Anon-ymous meetings, did so remarkably well (though when we drank in front of him, he looked like a man watching beautiful nude women parade by—just out of reach). He used a story that medical problems were the reason for his abstinence, and if pressed, he launched into an explanation so technical and boring that whoever had asked the question quickly regretted it. (Ever had an old-maid aunt who drones on incessantly about her aches, pains, and surgeries, complete with details and dates? Then you get the picture.)

How a Problem Can Develop

While it can sneak up on someone in a variety of ways, an undercover officer's drinking problem typically begins during a period when he must spend a large amount of time in bars. If he is not accustomed to drinking, he is going to suffer from a hangover the next day, but he returns the next night and does it all over again because it is his job. Heavy drinkers get used to hangovers; feeling sick in the morning becomes the norm, and after awhile, unless the pain is unusually severe, they hardly notice it. Drinking is a lot like exercise in this respect—the more you do it, the less it hurts. For awhile, at least.

Drinking is frequently part of the job and can carry over into your personal life. Be careful and find another area of law enforcement if problems seem to be developing. (Photo by Edward Hasbrook)

When this undercover officer has a night off, how do you think he decides to spend it? Well, he hasn't gotten to hang out with his cop friends for a long time, so he heads to the local "cop bar." This is the one place where he can take off his beard and be himself, and whether he's recognized it or not, he's developing a real fondness for that fuzzy feeling in his head. He's learned to operate efficiently while mildly intoxicated, and he believes that a little alcohol even helps him. It takes the edge off and facilitates getting into his undercover character. Besides, as he's already told himself, it's his job. (Remember when I talked about rationalization?)

Whether or not this imaginary undercover cop is a true, physically addicted alcoholic is not for me to determine. But even if he isn't, large amounts of alcohol on a regular basis never does anyone any good and has been known to do much harm. The edge that came off so easily with a couple of beers soon begins to require more. Then more, and more, and more. The line that separates the ability and inability to operate successfully under the influence of alcohol is thin. It will shrink quickly until it's anorexic.

I am not preaching abstinence. I simply want you to be aware that drinking undercover can aggravate a problem if it's already there. You should do some real soul-searching if you suspect that it could cause you difficulties. To me, there is no more fun, exciting, or rewarding area of law enforcement than undercover work. But writing speeding tickets or sitting behind a desk is preferable to sleeping in the gutter after you've lost your family, friends, and everything else that means anything in your life.

SEX

Okay, we've finished drinking, and now it's time for sex. Sex is an activity that most human beings enjoy. If you do not, skip this section and go on. Also, do not bother to introduce yourself to me should we ever meet. We probably have nothing in common.

While sex is fun, anyone with half a brain knows that sex with the wrong person, or at the wrong time, or in the wrong place, can lead to the biggest trouble this side of death. Nowhere is the wrong kind of sex more available than when you're working undercover.

I'm going to address the next few paragraphs from the male point of view for two reasons: first, as I explained earlier, that's still the accepted form when speaking of both genders. Second, male undercover officers seem to get themselves in far more trouble in this area than women. Never forget this basic truth: no one is immune to temptation all the time. Not you, not your partner, and not me. Before I end this chapter, I'll tell you a story that proves that I'm as susceptible to temptation as anyone else.

Temptation

Okay, let's face the facts. You're out there with the bad guys, and nobody knows who you are. You're not only using another name, you've got a whole different identity that will hold up if someone checks into it. In other words, unless you commit a major felony, you have the ability to do something and then disappear from the face of the earth without leaving a trace. This, in itself, can be an aphrodisiac. Added to this is the fact that you have been away from home for a considerable length of time. You have not been with your wife or girlfriend (or your whatever in this day and age) for a longer period of time than you prefer. Your "marital urge" is aroused. In other words, you're horny.

If you are hanging out with the bad guys, the bad girls are sure to be around, too. Is it necessary to tell you that having sex with someone who you may later have to testify against can have negative repercussions? I can hear the defense attorney now. "Detective Zipperman," he says, "Is it true that you slept with the defendant, Ms. Goesdown, on at least three occasions?"

"Uh . . . well . . . yeah, but that has nothing to do with the case."

"Thank you Detective. That will be all."

Put yourself in the jury box and decide if this would influence your decision. If you are single, you'll probably just lose the case and be transferred to the Animal Control division. If you're married, you stand to lose a lot more.

You're sitting there reading this, and you've become irritated with me because you've figured all this out yourself. You might fool around a little undercover, you're thinking, but you're certainly not stupid enough to do so with a potential defendant. If you take this attitude, I wish you luck and you are in my prayers. Prayer is the only thing that will save you, because you don't know who will turn out to be a defendant when all is said and done.

Sex With Defendants

Picture this: You're sitting in a hotel bar putting the final touches on a large cocaine buy. The dealer, Jack, wants to show his appreciation for your new business relationship, and the next thing you know, two of the most beautiful women you've ever seen appear at your table. Their names are Mona and Rona and, lo and behold, you've somehow entered that magical mystical world where dreams really do come true—they're both for you.

Some of you are shaking your heads in disbelief. You already know that the average woman you meet undercover isn't much of a temptation. She has never confronted a bar of soap or a can of deodorant and looks like she'd be lucky to get a date with the Elephant Man. That's true. But the operative phrase here is average. In order to have an average, half the group has to be above average, and a few have to be at the top, which means that there are exceptions to the foul-smelling, track-ridden, human tattoo canvases that immediately come to mind.

Jack throws the key to room 1256 across the table and tells you to have fun. He says he's in room 1122 and he'll meet you there with the dope in a couple of hours. Before you know it, you're upstairs living out all your fantasies, because Mona and Rona aren't in on the buy and there won't be a reason to subpoena them to court, right?

Wrong. Three hours later, the phone rings. You're exhausted beyond your wildest imagination, and you've got this incredibly moronic smile on your face as you roll from between your two new friends and grab the receiver.

"Listen, something unexpected just came up," Jack says, "I've got to leave, but I've stashed the stuff in my room. Rona and Mona have a key. Give them the money."

Your moronic smile fades fast. Your expression is still that of an imbecile—just not a happy one anymore. Your case on Jack isn't going to be as cut and dried as before, but that's the least of your worries. The buy suddenly includes the two women you are watching slip back into their garter belts. That means warrants for their arrest. It also means that there's a good chance that some sexual acts you'd just as soon no one knew you could even think of may come out in court. Mona and Rona are going to tell their attorney all about the last three hours, and don't think for a second that he won't go into detail. The two women might even testify themselves. If your wife or girl-friend doesn't find out, then my prayers for you will have been answered, because an act of God is what it will take.

Your problems may be even worse than you think. You use tape recorders and video cameras. Well, Jack knows where Radio Shack is, too. If he had even the least suspicion that you might be a cop, Radio Shack might be exactly where he stopped before he met you in the bar. Is it your imagination, or do you really hear a humming sound coming from behind the mirror across from the hotel bed? The defense attorney will keep the master tape. One copy will go to the district attorney's office, and another to your chief. And don't be surprised to find your wife watching the family VCR someday when you get home—for the last time.

Sex With Informants
Sex with informants is every bit as dangerous as it is

with defendants. Today's informant may well be tomorrow's defendant. (Remember the mercenary informant who planted the marijuana under the back seat of the Volkswagen?) Informants do not come from Sunday school rolls, and they will turn on you if it is to their advantage. Go to bed with one of them and you are no longer in control. They are.

You, naturally, would never be that stupid, right? Would it surprise you that one of the smartest undercover cops I've ever known has been paying child support to a former informant for nearly 18 years? "Gus" was spending more time with his female informant than he was his wife. One night the moon was full and there was music in the air. The informant was a clean, attractive, and mostly decent woman who had gotten busted when she got involved with the wrong people. Gus made the same mistake by getting involved with her. She got pregnant. Gus was lucky, though; he was able to salvage his marriage. But I can't help guessing that he's paid for the affair with a lot more than money over the years.

Given the right time, the right place, the right set of supplementary circumstances, and the right body chemistry between two people, and even you can be felled, you oak you. Having sex with informants has broken up many a marriage. Children, homes, stocks, bonds, and everything else of value has been lost.

The Undercover Life-Style

Why do many undercover officers fall for these obvious traps? In addition to the normal human sex drive, there is pressure to live loosely undercover. James Bond, Mike Hammer, and other fictional characters have created an image that many cops feel they must emulate. They view themselves as tough, two-fisted, hard-drinking, love-'em-and-leave-'em womanizers of the silver screen. To make matters worse, they hear stories about real officers who actually pull it off.

You will probably spend more time with informants than you do with your wife. Be very careful. Undercover cops are human, and humans develop relationships. This . . .

. . . can lead to this. (Photos by Edward Hasbrook)

Once upon a time there was an undercover cop I'll call "Baxter." Baxter had a reputation as both a top operative and a lady's man. He was big, strong, handsome, and as close to being a real live Dirty Harry as I ever met. Whether he was working or not, I never saw Baxter without a beautiful woman on his arm. Many officers were jealous of him. (Me? Well, maybe just a little.) Some officers tried to follow his sexual lead, but most got caught at one time or another. Baxter and his reputation lived on.

One day Baxter started running with an extremely good looking, intelligent, and devious female informant I'll call "Trudy." To make a long story short, he fell in love with her. Baxter was single, so this was not going to cause him any problems with respect to marriage. The fact that Trudy was doing a tremendous job meant the charges on her were likely to be dismissed, and Baxter wouldn't face any heat at the department about dating a felon, either. It seemed that old Baxter had pulled it off again.

Love is a wonderful thing, but as in all relationships, Baxter and Trudy eventually had a little lover's spat. Trudy took it more seriously than Baxter and told the gang of righteously bad thieves and drug dealers they'd been running with who her boyfriend really was. One day Baxter was run off the road, shots were fired, and he took one in the spine. He's paralyzed from the waist down now, drawing medical retirement, and fewer officers are jealous of him than used to be.

A Confession

I promised a confession, and the time for it has come. As I said, I'm as susceptible to weak moments as anyone else. Here goes.

"Sally" was 22, had long blond hair, soft blue eyes the color of the ocean, and the smoothest skin you could imagine. She was intelligent, funny, creative, and the kind of girl you wanted to put your arm around and say, even though you knew she didn't need it, "Hey, don't worry, I'll take care of you." She'd been arrested for simple marijuana possession—usually not a severe enough bust to convince anyone to turn informant, but Sally was a pharmaceutical student at the local university, and any drug conviction meant she wouldn't get her license after graduation.

Late one hot summer afternoon, Sally and I were at her apartment waiting until it was time to go make a buy. We were drinking wine, and she got up to put a record on the stereo. When she did, her short, cutoff jeans rode up even higher, showing me that the skin of her upper thighs and hips was every bit as smooth as that of her face. I remember gulping my wine a little faster as I turned my head away and reminded myself that the feelings I was having could cause more trouble than I needed.

As soft music drifted from the stereo, I felt the wine began to relax me. The only other sound was the constant, soothing murmur of the air conditioner in the window, and I found myself beginning to rationalize an affair with Sally. I didn't even know if she was interested, but what if she was? She wasn't a drug user, really. She'd already told me that the marijuana she'd been caught with belonged to a friend, and that she didn't smoke it herself. Even if she had tried it a few times, how many college kids hadn't? Besides, she was about to graduate with a degree and become a pharmacist. She was a professional. She even had a job lined up.

The curtains had been drawn back from the window, and two aged elm trees stood just outside, their branches swaying gently in the hot breeze. Twilight fell over the living room, and the branches began to cast dark, dancing shadows across the walls.

The wine made me warm, and I reached up to loosen the collar of my shirt. When I did, I saw Sally staring at me, those crystal blue eyes answering my earlier question. Yes, she was interested. We both turned away quickly. Neither of us said a word, but in that brief moment we both knew that we had looked at each other in a new way.

I tried to keep my eyes on the floor, but it was impossible. Finally, I looked up and she was staring at me again. This time, our eyes locked, and neither of us turned away.

Then the doorbell rang. "Tom," a fellow undercover officer who was working with us on the deal, walked in. We all left, did the deal, went our separate ways, and that's my story.

What? You were expecting something better than that? Something more revealing? Something where I admitted to giving into temptation like the other officers I told you about? Are you crazy? Having sex with defendants or informants is stupid, but admitting in print to doing such things is insane.

PART 6

WRAPPING IT ALL UP

CHAPTER 19
Testifying in Court

Baseball scores mean nothing until the last out of the ninth inning; no football team was ever congratulated for playing three good quarters and choking in the fourth; heavyweight champions who win the first 14 rounds but get knocked out in the 15th still lose the belt; and even though Japan and Germany won the first part of World War II they still lost the war.

"It ain't over 'til it's over," Yogi Berra said. Nowhere does that statement hold more true than in undercover work. You can be the best undercover performer in the world, but if you can't tell a judge and jury successfully about what you did, your efforts are a total waste of time.

Many cases are plea bargained these days, and you won't even get to the preliminary hearing on most, but in others you will take the stand so it pays to know how to do so productively. Your courtroom testimony will not be much different from any other law enforcement officer's, and there are good books and training classes available to assist you in general courtroom testimony. Therefore, I'm going to look primarily at the peculiarities you will face when testifying as an undercover officer.

REFRESH YOUR MEMORY

Before you arrive at the courthouse, refresh your memory concerning the details of the specific case. Court dates that involve undercover cases, particularly those that are drug-related, have a tendency to be continued time after time, dragging on even longer than normal criminal cases. Review your notes, reports, audio and videotape recordings, and all other evidence. You will have undertaken many other undercover assignments since the one that led to the arrest of the defendant in the courtroom now, and the details of the case will have faded from your mind.

One of the first undercover drug buys I ever made was from some pond scum that had somehow assimilated into human form. I'll call him "Pond" so you don't forget his origin. The relatively small buy went down in a motel room, and we planned to arrest Pond at a later date when we were able to round up several of his buddies from the lagoon. In the meantime, Pond left the state and got arrested in Utah. He was tried, convicted, and sentenced there. We put a hold on him so that when his time was up he'd be extradited back to my state to face our charges, nine years later.

Pond was a righteously dangerous character, and even though the charges were old and small, the district attorney preferred that he be sent to our penitentiary rather than have him return to the primordial slime from which he'd risen. A preliminary hearing was docketed, I was subpoenaed, and when I finally remembered who Pond was I began to feel like my great uncle with Alzheimer's. Finally, I found my old notebook, dusted it off, and went to work. To be honest, I was shocked. The notes spawned a domino-like chain of recollections that made it seem as though the buy had taken place last week, and I testified as well as I would have if it had been a fresh case.

But I am hardly unique. For most of you, merely reviewing notes and other evidence will be enough to help you recall all pertinent data. If you find yourself having trouble, refer to the chapter on developing memory. Grab a few books on the subject, and practice. Visualize the scenario. Close your eyes and go over the sequence of events of the case in your mind. Relive everything that happened. Don't skip this critically important step in preparation, and don't rush it. Time invested preparing to testify pays big conviction dividends after you've left the stand.

PHYSICAL APPEARANCE

Your physical appearance in court is every bit as important as what you say. Although juries know you have to look like a criminal when you go undercover, they expect to see you looking like a cop in court. If your appearance is seedier than the defendant's you've got one strike against you as soon as you walk in the door. Like any officer, you want to present yourself as neatly and professionally as possible, but this can get a little tricky when you're doing a lot of undercover work. The general public understands that you sometimes grow long, unruly hair and beards, wear earrings, dress like counterculture figures, and do your best to look like the criminals with whom you must associate. Perhaps they also know that sometimes you do not bathe for a few days in order to fit in with the animal element. They know it, but letting them see it is never a good idea.

Jurors are human beings like anyone else. Regardless of how hard attorneys try to find jury members who have no preconceived notions and prejudices, they always fail because people completely free of such frailties do not exist. What the jurors see in court will influence their judgment. If you walk like a duck and talk like a duck . . .

The jury will be trying to decide whether they should believe you or the defendant. This means that, consciously or

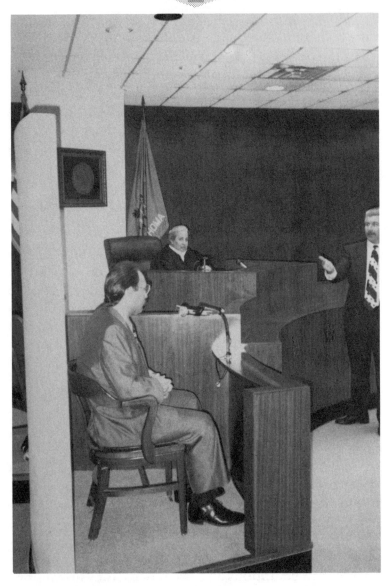

Clean up your act when it's time to take the stand. The jury will be more impressed with the professional you than your undercover identity. (Photo by Edward Hasbrook)

subconsciously, they will be comparing the two of you. The greasy maggot that looked like Don King having a bad hair day, sported a flea-infested beard that bore witness to everything he'd eaten for three weeks, and wore clothes that looked like they were donated to Goodwill by the Marquis de Sade when you busted him is not going to look that way by the time he gets to court. He'll be clean shaven, wearing a new suit that his attorney picked out, and looking like a little angel on his way to Vacation Bible School.

Hate the guy if you must, but learn a lesson from him. He's done exactly what he should do in his situation, and you should too.

Witness Jekyl and Undercover Cop Hyde

There are a few conflicts undercover cops face in regard to court appearance that don't affect their straight brothers. For example, if you've been working on a junk bond deal, you've probably been hanging around penthouse offices and drinking martini lunches with a guy named Chip Jr., and you won't have to change clothes before you head for the courthouse. But if you've been running with the Crips and have earrings in both nostrils, it's time for the diamond studs to come out. You can stick them back in after the gavel comes down and the defendant is on his way to the penitentiary.

Well, here's the kind of little crinkle that makes things interesting, which occurs more often than not. The junk bond case is old news. For the last several months you've been working on this really huge ganja buy from a Cayman Islander named Raoul. You've let your hair grow down to your shoulders, and you've got a beard that hides your navel when you don't wear a shirt. You've already met with Raoul twice to set things up, and the deal is supposed to go down in two days.

The problem is that Chip Jr. goes to trial on the junk bond deal the day before the ganja buy. The old Chipster's retained a high-dollar attorney, and rumor has it they've seated exactly the kind of jurors they want: high class and a little bit snooty, perhaps. What this boils down to is that the men and women in the jury box will be more sympathetic than usual to a clean-cut little shrimp like Chipper, and they will turn their noses straight up when you walk in looking like Keith Richards of the Rolling Stones. So how can you look like a stockbroker one day and return to your usual maggot self the next? You can't. Not unless your hair and beard grow like the grass in my backyard.

As you prepare for court, keep in mind what you want to say to the members of the jury through your appearance: "Yes, I'm one of those undercover spy-guys like you see on TV, but if it weren't for the job, I'd look just like you." Compromise and compensation are the names of the game, here. Trim your beard a little, then steal some of your wife's setting gel so you don't look like Rasputin after the tornado. Tie your hair back in a ponytail, and if it's long enough, stick it down the back of your collar. It's more important now than ever that your shoes are spit shined, and make sure the creases in the slacks of your gray "banker" suit are pressed straight. The cuffs and collar of your best white Oxford cloth shirt should be well starched, and pay careful attention to that tie you got from your mother-in-law for Christmas—the beer you spilled on it after court last week needs to be cleaned off.

Another way to compromise is to just go ahead and shave the beard and get a haircut. Bad guys sometimes do these things too, you know. What you have to ask yourself is whether or not this drastic change in your appearance will make Raoul too uneasy to go through with the deal. If you choose this route, as always, you'll need a reason for what you've done. Something like, "I had to go to court on my divorce," or, "My probation officer's being an asshole."

Is Raoul the kind of guy who will buy stories like these? Don't ask me—you're the one who knows him. To decide which route you will take in solving the problem of appearance, as in all the other iffy areas of undercover work, you must evaluate your targeted criminal and the overall situation, and then make the best decision you can with the facts that are at your disposal. Don't expect to come up with any magic 100-percent solutions; they don't exist. Make your decision, and then don't look back. Like Satchel Page said, "Something might be gaining on you."

TAKING THE STAND

As a witness in a preliminary hearing you must establish and maintain three different relationships: one with the judge, one with the prosecutor, and one with the defense counsel. If the case goes to trial, the fourth and most important relationship of all is added—the jury.

It is helpful if the judge, jury, and prosecutor decide that they like you, but not essential. What is important is that they trust you. (Keep in mind that for many shallow people "like" and "trust" are interchangeable.) Since the prosecutor already assumes that you are telling the truth, your goal is to make the judge and jury do the same. The attorney for the defense is a little different. He probably knows his client is guilty, but his job is to make it look like you are the one who should spend the next 20 years making license tags. He's going to treat you like you are lying through your teeth, regardless.

Judges
Judges are like any other group of people: there are good ones and bad ones, but most fall somewhere in between. Some judges maneuvered their way onto the bench because they were unsuccessful attorneys and needed a steady paycheck. Others are there because they really believe in what they're doing and don't care that they could be making 10 times as much money in private practice. Some judges are confident enough to be friendly.

(I've downed a good deal of beer with a few of them, and on one occasion I even got into a bar fight with one at my side. His Honor and I won and got out of there as the sirens began to near. He could hold his own too—not nearly the wimp you'd expect a judge to be.) Others use their position to intimidate others. Some judges have brilliant legal minds, while it's difficult to understand how others ever graduated from law school. A few have been on the bench so long that they're as senile as that uncle of mine with Alzheimer's I mentioned earlier.

Your job, if you want to win your case, is to determine what type of judge you're dealing with and behave accordingly. In general, treat all judges the same when court is in session. Be respectful (some judges prefer subservience, but you have to draw the line somewhere), and be polite. Address the judge as Your Honor, Sir, or Ma'am, and look directly at the bench when you speak to the court. If you establish a good relationship with the person in the robes, it will be to your advantage.

Attorneys and judges plea bargain more criminal cases and resolve more civil suits and other court-related issues over lunches and golf games than they do in court. Likewise, it is away from the courthouse where you establish an individual relationship with a judge. I am not suggesting that you drop to your knees and pucker your lips. My ego has always prevented me from brownnosing, and since you're an Explorer, yours should too. But if you bump into a truly obnoxious judge at the local coffee shop, you can be polite and respectful to his position, if not him. You will more than likely face him again someday in court, and that is his kingdom. The little potentate has a thousand ways to screw you around if he's disgraceful enough to use them, and some judges are every bit that ignoble. On the other hand, you may find a judge with whom you can become friends. If so, that's an ace up your sleeve, and if you can get your cases steered his way, you're already one up in the game.

Prosecutors

Although you hope that the prosecutor respects, trusts, and perhaps even likes you, this is not always the case. Chances are that if you don't like him, he doesn't think much of you either, but that doesn't mean you shouldn't do your best to establish a good working relationship with him.

Undoubtedly the best prosecuting attorney I ever knew was a man I'll call "Joe." Joe was in his 50s, partially disabled, diabetic, and had every other health problem listed in the Merck manual. He was also arrogant, condescending, egocentric, rude, slovenly, and obnoxious, but good Lord in Heaven above, when the man limped into that courtroom with his cane he was in his element. Joe became a completely different person in the courtroom. Actually, he became whatever type of person it took to win the case. He could sense exactly what questions to ask witnesses, when to ask them, and how they should be phrased to make the good guys look better and the bad guys look like Satan. Closing arguments were his forte. I will never forget a case where he compared the defendant to Lucifer and me to "our crucified Savior who gave his life for mankind." (Do not be confused—there is far less resemblance than there should be.) He was Clarence Darrow and Sir Lawrence Olivier rolled into one, and he won his cases.

Although my personal feelings about Joe as a human being sometimes bordered on loathing, he had my respect, and I went out of my way to get along with him. If you want to win your cases, you would be wise to do the same with any "Joes" you encounter.

Juries

Throughout this book, I've been making up names like "Joe" and "Tom" for real people. Now, I find it necessary to fabricate an entire fraternal order. You'll see why in a minute.

Shortly after I undertook my first law enforcement job (I was a county jailer, but that story deserves a whole book in itself), I was persuaded by the sheriff to join an international lodge. This lodge is a fine organization and does a lot of good things, and I'm not putting it down, but I found out very quickly that it was not for me. (Among other things, I was the youngest member by about 40 years.) In any case, I went through what I considered to be a pretty silly initiation ceremony, complete with funny costumes, secret handshakes, and secret signs. At the conclusion, one of the members presented me with a lodge lapel pin. (I was a little disappointed—I'd been hoping for a secret decoder ring.) I thanked him, pinned it to my jacket, paid my membership dues, and haven't been back since.

Several months later, I had been moved to narcotics work and was sitting in the courtroom preparing to take the stand in a drug case. I noticed an elderly member of the jury staring at me. As I watched him out of the corner of my eye, it became evident that he wasn't looking at my face, but rather somewhere on my chest. So I looked down to see if I was wearing some of the Big Mac I'd had for lunch. Everything looked clean. The juror, however, just kept staring. Now he was squinting as if trying to make out some small detail. So I looked down again, and my eyes fell on the lodge pin that was still in my lapel. I looked back to the juror and saw that he was wearing one, too. So I gave the lodge's secret hand sign, and he flashed me the secret return signal. I didn't know if the rest of the jury would believe my testimony, but at that point I had one jury member on my side for sure.

The point is, establish trust with the members of the jury and the judge through whatever means present themselves.

Defense Attorneys

There is one great mistake that many cops make on the stand and are not even aware of it. It is a passive mistake rather than an overt one—a state of mind. That is, they walk up to the stand and take their seat under the assumption that the defense attorney is smarter than they are.

We have been coerced into believing this because the

counsel for the defense has successfully completed law school, passed the bar exam, and makes far more money than we do. Therefore, he must be more intelligent and capable of making us look like fools with his questions. If this is a problem for you, you've got to get over it. The truth of the matter is that although you may be outgunned in the brains department once in awhile, usually you and the defense attorney are on a much closer intellectual plane that you might think.

The Intimidation Game

When you face cross-examination, you are in a fight. The weapons used are words rather than fists, guns, knives, or bombs, but it is a fight nonetheless. Remember that fights are most often won or lost before the battle even begins, because one side has confidence and the other does not. One fighter knows he will win and behaves as a winner. His opponent is intimidated, prepares for loss, and then follows that plan. If you believe that you will be defeated, rest assured you will be.

This phenomena can be observed quite distinctly in dogs. Put a German Shepherd puppy in a backyard with a fully grown Chihuahua, and the German Shepherd will fear the small snapping animal long after he has grown to the point where the little beast wouldn't even make a decent breakfast. Unless some random event takes place that changes the Shepherd's beliefs, he will always allow the Chihuahua to bully him into submission.

We, as human beings, have the advantage of not having to wait for random events, because we can consciously change our beliefs and attitudes. Think of all the inept attorneys you know. (They are out there, and every officer knows at least one.) They are the fodder of courthouse anecdotes and are ridiculed not only by their more adept colleagues, but by police officers and everyone else with whom they deal.

When I was a young officer, attorneys frightened me.

Then a friend told me about an incident that helped me realize that a law degree is certainly not a direct link to superior mental power. My friend owned a clothing store, and during a sale to get rid of merchandise that had been gathering dust for years, he sold a pair of size 15 shoes to an attorney named "Pete" with whom we were both acquainted.

"Pete," my friend said as he rang up the $5 charge on the cash register, "I didn't know anyone in your family had feet that big."

"Well, they don't," the attorney said without a trace of embarrassment. "But five bucks—it's such a good deal!"

This man had graduated from law school, passed the bar, and made a relatively good living. Of course, such incompetent and often flat stupid attorneys are the exception rather than the rule, but this example should give you a start in gaining confidence on the witness stand. What you must realize, if you don't already, is that the ability to pass law school tests and the skill of putting an education to practical use do not always go hand in hand.

Tell the Truth

When you testify, if you tell the truth, there is no way the defense counsel can "trip you up." This practical argument harmonizes well with the ethical and moral reasons for truthfulness under oath. A large part of your life as an undercover officer is spent telling people that you are someone who you are not. For strictly personal reasons, this makes telling the truth even more important for you than the straight officer— you need to know that you are an honest person.

So, how do you answer the defense attorney who turns to the jury as he asks, "Mr. John Jacob Watkins, did you not, in fact, falsely identify yourself to the defendant as one Mickey Jordan, and then claim to be a drug dealer from Chicago, Illinois?"

"I was portraying the part of Mickey Jordan," you should say.

"So," the attorney will reply, "You lied to my client?"

"No, sir, not at all. Certainly no more than the professional actor who portrays a character on stage or on film. I was creating the illusion that I was a criminal in order to find out if your client was a drug dealer." And if you can get it in, add, "And he was."

The defense attorney is not going to like this very much. He was hoping you'd squirm around and finally say something like, "Well, yeah . . . I guess I lied but—" at which point he'd cut you off with another question. But since you didn't fall for his ploy, he may resort to another tired, old lawyer trick. Interrupting you at about the time you say, "I was creating an illusion . . . " he will shout in your face, "Did you lie to my client or not?" then order you to, "Answer the question, yes or no!"

But guess what boys and girls? You don't have to. No matter how much defense attorneys would love to have the power to give you orders like that, they don't. No one in the courtroom can force you to answer yes or no except the judge. That doesn't mean the defense won't try, but don't let it intimidate you. Remember to keep your answers relatively short. If you get too wordy, you may find yourself in a position that I was once in after committing that sin.

"Answer the question yes or no!" the defense attorney screamed.

I proceeded to repeat verbatim what I had just said, ignoring his order.

Then the judge told me to answer the question. This was a problem because the person in the robes can do this.

I turned to the bench and said, "Your Honor, I took an oath to tell the truth, the whole truth, and nothing but the truth. If I answer this complex question in the manner the defense has requested, it will be misleading to both the court and the jury. I will not be telling the whole truth, and I will violate an oath that I took very seriously."

The judge understood this and changed her order to, "Then please keep your answers as short as possible."

I should have been doing this already, but I wasn't.

When you are on the stand, get in everything you can, but try to condense your answers into the fewest possible words. As always there are exceptions, but as a rule you should not use more than three to five sentences.

Steer Clear of Problem Areas

What I'm about to say may seem like a contradiction after talking about telling the truth, but it is not a discrepancy; it is a way of ensuring that the whole truth is seen. Steer the defense away from problem areas in your case.

All undercover cases have a problem area. I won't get into specifics, because I have no intention of giving unprincipled defense attorneys any more tools to distort cases than they already have, but if you have worked undercover, you know that every time you put on your beard some minor occurrence happens that could be misconstrued in court. This is the way life is; the retelling of some events changes their entire significance. No matter how hard you try to explain what the event meant at the time it occurred and why it appears to hold a different implication in court, you will not be successful. I am not talking about incidents that would prove the defendant innocent—if you know the defendant is innocent, you should have dropped the charges long ago. I am talking about silly little things that can damage the rest of the evidence and may lead to justice not being served.

The answer you give a defense attorney often determines the next question he asks. If you suspect that his line of questioning is approaching a problem area, it is best to answer in a way that guides him in a new direction. Since each problem area is unique, your answer must be just as unique. As you do when you are undercover, you must stay alert and think on your feet. You will be entering a gray area in where the line between "steering" the defense counsel and purposely misleading the jury is sometimes thin. Stay on the moral side of it.

This will not work with all attorneys. Undoubtedly the

finest trial lawyer I ever faced was a gentleman by the name of Harold Singer. Harold was a man who had the respect of both the law community and the community in general and possessed the sharpest legal mind I've ever encountered. I tried to steer Harold away from a problem area once, and I could almost see radar antennas sprout from his head. He patiently let me finish what I was saying, then went right back to the line of questioning he'd been on. Each attempt to turn him in a new direction brought him closer to what I didn't want to talk about, and I began to wonder if he had the ability to read my mind. To this day, I'm not completely convinced that the man didn't possess magical powers. The normal pretestimony butterflies became giant hummingbirds beating their wings in my stomach each time I faced Harold after that day. But even he could not trip me up, because I told the truth.

USING NOTES ON THE STAND

Some officers bring their notes on the stand with them, and this is certainly an acceptable practice. If you do this, however, the defense has a right to examine the material and question you about it, and it may give the enemy more ammunition than he already has to mislead both judge and jury. Unless I'm testifying in a case in which complex statistics are pertinent, I always prefer to study my notes and then rely on my memory. A desire to avoid aiding the defense is part of the reason. I'll never forget the officer I once watched squirm in his seat as he confessed that the phone number jotted in the margin of his notebook had nothing to do with the case. It belonged to an attractive hooker he'd met during the investigation.

CHAPTER 20

Opening the Door

I learned the undercover trade by working with many excellent officers. I learned the most, however, from a guy named Sid Cookerly. Sid used to say that he never put anyone in the penitentiary. They did that themselves—he just opened the door for them.

If you are new to undercover work, you are about to start opening that penitentiary door for some bad guys, and if you are a seasoned undercover officer, you have opened the door a time or two already. You are already familiar with most aspects of undercover work, and you may have found that *Going Undercover* contains certain points, or even some general philosophy, with which you disagree. There's nothing wrong with that—undercover work is an art, not a science, and there's plenty of room for different opinions. What works well for one officer may not work for another, and what begets results in one setting can be disastrous in others. Only one rule is set in stone: if it works, use it. If it doesn't, get rid of it as fast as you can and find something that does. It is my hope, however, that I have passed on something useful from my experiences that you can add to your alternate personality and overall approach to the subject. It is also my hope that you have enjoyed reading *Going Undercover*, you have found it entertaining as well as educational, and you will keep it handy so you can refer to it from time to time.

Some key points to keep in mind are:

1) I've examined the types of people who enjoy undercover work and are apt to make good clandestine operatives, as well as those who aren't likely to take to it naturally and will be starting with one strike against them. I've called them Explorers and Homesteaders, and if any Homesteaders made it all the way to the end of this book, perhaps you are not Homesteaders after all. (On the other hand, you guys always finish what you start—whether it makes sense to do so or not.)

2) You have created an undercover identity and added to it a specific character with a personality that is flexible enough to work in a wide variety of environments. Your character should have some idea what to wear, what to drive, what to order at the bar, and how to act within the different cultural and economic atmospheres in which he will function.

3) By practicing the exercises in Chapter 6, you have become acquainted with your new identity and become confident that you can convince people that you are who and what you claim to be. If you still feel uncomfortable after completing these drills, keep practicing them or create new ones of your own. Better yet, enroll in an acting class, get some experience in public speaking, or audition for a part in a community theater production.

4) Keep in mind that while most people do not pay close attention to others, when you are doing a drug deal,

talking to an armed robber, or posing as a hit man, you are the center of your audience's attention. Your target will be watching you vigilantly and looking for any discrepancies in what you say and do.

5) The key to any undercover operation is your informant and how he is handled—with you in control at all times. Plan each operation as thoroughly as possible, utilizing all the information at your disposal and realizing that you will not have complete control once your beard is on. Control what you can, but be ready for surprises. Be prepared to think on your feet, and never, ever let them see you sweat.

6) If you find it advantageous to create the illusion of a robbery, burglary, murder, or any other crime, go over every detail of what can go wrong. Keep in mind that you are walking a thin legal line, and that you cannot help but miss some of the potential traps. Inevitably, something will not go as you had planned. Remember that you are taking big chances, so keep the human risk factor as low as possible.

7) Develop your memory and learn to cover the mistakes you may make while undercover.

8) Make sure that the weapons you choose to carry are in perfect working order and that you are skilled in their use. When you are undercover, you are dealing with the bad guys at very close range. The type of physical conflicts you are likely to encounter may not give you time to draw a weapon no matter what you are carrying. Think of all the trouble your wife will have trying to get your life insurance company to pay off. Make it easy on her. If you are not a well-trained unarmed fighter, consider taking classes in a practical self-defense-oriented martial art.

9) Remember that your surveillance/backup team will never arrive at the scene in time to help you if you get in trouble. It's you against the world, and you must not operate under the fantasy that the cavalry

will ride in to save you. You are on your own.

10) Keep your eyes open and be able to recognize the physical, legal, political, and personal traps that are waiting to ensnare you. You are human and therefore imperfect. Given the right set of circumstances and events, you too can fall.

11) When the undercover work on a case is over, and the criminal has become a defendant, present yourself properly in court. Tell the truth, the whole truth, and nothing but the truth—but don't be afraid to guide the defense attorney away from problem areas. You are just as intelligent, professional, and capable as the man who keeps screaming that you are lying about his client—don't let him intimidate you.

Undercover work can be the most exciting and rewarding area in all law enforcement. It can also be the most frustrating. It can lead to a feeling of true accomplishment when the jury foreman says, "guilty," and it can make you want to slit your wrists when the defendant you worked on for two years is released on a technicality. Undercover work can be a route to self-fulfillment, or it can lead to total ruin. Only you can decide which it will be for you.

If all cops are brothers and sisters, then the men and women of undercover work are identical if not Siamese twins. The bond created when wearing a beard with a fellow officer is as strong as any in the human experience. My partner of five years, Mark Bray, and I were closer than brothers. When I lost him, I lost part of myself.

Now go open that door for some bad guys. Good luck, and have fun. Mark and I will be with you in spirit.

About the Author

In his 14 years as a police officer, Jerry VanCook served as a Narcotics Investigator and Deputy Sheriff for the Garfield County Sheriff's Department, an Undercover Intelligence Officer for the Multi-County Intelligence Task Force in Oklahoma, and a Special Operations Agent for the Oklahoma State Bureau of Investigation. Much of his experience includes undercover work in narcotics, stolen property, murder conspiracy, and other crimes.

Before embarking on his police career, he was a martial arts instructor and is presently on the Council of Advisors for the National Jiyushinkai AikiBudo Association and a member of the Okinawan Karate-do Association.

He became a professional writer in 1987 and has written 18 action/adventure novels under a pseudonym. He is also currently a contributing editor for *Trail's End* magazine.